Proud to be Naked

**please feel guilt free writing
any where in this book –
once you have bought it**

note page

Best wishes on your path. Carolyn Joel Elva

Proud to be Naked

go barefoot on the road
to self discovery

carolyn joel elva

illustrations **myrna shoa**

published by
Truck Stop Spirituality 2000

Truck Stop Spirituality 2000
an imprint of Magdalena Productions
on the streets of New York or London

email - create2001@aol.com

Published by Truck Stop Spirituality 2000
14 Shrewsbury Road
London, W2 5PR

ISBN   0 9538820 1 2

Printed and bound in Great Britain by –
The Book Factory
Telephone – 020 7700 1000
Fax – 020 7700 3569

Cover design inspired by Paris of Greek myths, art works by
Rubens and Donatello, and others who appreciated beauty,
unconcealed.

To

the flying sisters

and the men and women

who have shared their stories around my

campfire

and are my family

note page

Forward

Why I wrote this book, now?

Several years ago I decided to go back and study the fathers of psychoanalysis Sigmund Freud and Carl Jung, to understand where our techniques of therapy at the end of the 20th century have come from.   There is a debate about the nature, methods, and value in conventional therapy which I have entered.

I believe it was their methods of research and **their deep need to know about themselves through self analysis** which made Freud, and Jung, so valuable to us as examples today.   They found their way through actions, not words alone.

They remain an inspiration - to look inward for the answers to our deepest needs. Freud and Jung would urge us to find our own paths, as they did. It is with this spirit that I have written the book.

note page

Contents

What else will you encounter on your quest?

pause here

Practical applications and examples

another pause

Background of the theories　285

Various paths others have taken - *(you can do it alone with occasional support)*

Take A DEEP BREATH

(Please note that he or she may be used in a non gender specific way in the text.)

illustrations

self Analysis -

Introduction

100 years ago...

Freud and Jung studied themselves for several years, like painters who repeatedly do self portraits because the subject is always available and they keep seeing more each time. They called this **self analysis**. A painter can sell her collection of self portraits. However, it's not so easy to make a profession out of self analysis.

So, although, self analysis was good enough for them to uncover their inner selves, without being taught, Freud and Jung decided to form schools and turned their backs on self analysis as a valid method on its own -for others. Psychoanalysis as a self perpetuating profession was born.

Today our thoughts, words, and images of how we see ourselves remain influenced by Freudian slips, Oedipal tales, and archetypes, all highlighted during the late 19th century.

The model for self discovery in the 20th century was based on the intense dedication and research of Freud and Jung into themselves.

In this book I explain the importance of 21st century action analysis for each of us.

For those readers who want more of the history of analysis. I then return to the legacy of Freud and Jung and the artistic therapies that developed later during the 20th century.

You will learn **skills** that will release you from the taboos and ties that bind you to habits of thinking and behaviour, learned early in life which you no longer need. These unnecessary ties and habits in your behaviour are the metaphorical dragons of legend, that you can overcome.

As you observe your choices and take a fresh look at your patterned responses, your thinking will expand and you will be calm as you face difficulties.

As you accept that what you say, what you do, and what you choose not to do, are all part of the unique person you are, **meaningless worries will slip away.** You will achieve this by realizing that **you have a choice** - to be still, not to be angry, not to go down a particular road. You will see that you want to do what you are doing, most of the time or you would not be doing it.

This is a leap in how you see yourself, and those around you.   It frees you from blaming and from discontent.

There are as many ways to face or hide from problems as there are techniques to provide answers. So, in this maze you may need information and want support, occasionally, from someone who has been down the road before you.   But, like those dedicated researchers, Freud and Jung, you can do it alone, if you need to enough.

Wanting to enough is the key.

Bearing in mind Jung's, somewhat contradictory, admonition, that I will only learn by sailing my own ship, I have my own philosophical and creative approach, which I will try to convey to you. I call it

Action Analysis.

Experience the process for yourself and make it your own method of self discovery, and liberation psychology.

There are several valuable tools in action analysis, artistic expression is one. Observation of your actions and choices not to act is another, as is analysis of the words you choose to say or to leave out.

Myths and stories from around the world are valuable to study, as mirrors placed at different angles.

Through symbol and metaphor they help you see clearly the prominent role of doing and not doing in your life and the lives of others.

Imagine yourself as the heroine or hero in the myth of your choice.   You will notice that, although the gods may mutter in disapproval at what you do, in the end it is their deeds that will destroy you, or uplift you.

From Zeus and Hera, of the ancient Greeks, to the Old Testament God and his bet with Lucifer about Job, it was the acts of these gods and the corresponding acts of the people they were testing which were crucial.   Faust says it.

The deed is all.

Throughout the book there are clues to the paths I have taken.   The joy comes from discovering your own path as you set off, stumble, or race ahead, on a heroic quest for transformation, hopefully always within sight of at least one fool and joker, and other wise travellers.

One of these joker, jester, fool characters I will refer to in the book is *Nasrudin*, famous in tales from the eastern Mediterranean to Afghanistan, and seen in most world tales in some guise.

Nasrudin is a universal mirror for our follies and wisdom.   See him, you see yourself. He is a fool who is not a fool. He can kid the king and still keep his head. He is a beacon aiming point blank at our mad stances, which we see as quite normal. He is our guide in this book.

START HERE

Action Analysis is a way to catch yourself and fundamentally change how you experience every nagging worry which keeps you awake, as well as preventing serious depression.

Action analysis is **simple**. You take responsibility for your life now. You clarify your outlook on life by observing your choices to act or not to act, and stop beating yourself up for choices you make.

It may seem unusual to focus on what you are not doing, but it is like recognising the equality of negative space in paintings, which is also created by the painter. When you choose to go to a film it means you are choosing not to do a range of other things.

Not walking to work is a choice just like the painted shape between the fingers is a choice by the painter.   It may look to an observer as though it just happened, but it is a considered part of the picture, and of who you are.

You begin with **Action**, which is a choice
you make not to be idle.   It's your life
force calling attention to itself.   It's
how you know you are not dead.
It's also how you find a lost coin in the
street, a lover, a new life.

ACTion is a
choice you make
not to be idle.

Action shifts your mood. Looking at your actions, you see what it is you really want to do, and what you do out of fear, greed, necessity, habit, or some impulse you are still unaware of.

It is through your actions, plus unknown factors, that you will change what you can, and accept that as a conscious evolutionary victory. To look at yourself in this way means you have a deep and urgent **need to know.**

Why would you want to look at yourself with this microscope? NECESSITY.

Major events and crises of a physical, emotional, or spiritual nature create a necessity to examine your life. The effects of births, deaths, and illnesses, as well as love, marriage, separation, divorce, or career moves, provide the stimulus to ask questions.

You learn to cope with changes, or you go under emotionally, and perhaps physically and financially as well. You will find that necessity causes new areas in your character to develop and you will surprise yourself at all the things you can do.

Personal changes due to age can compound the effect of illness or loss, but these are valuable spurs of nature to keep you moving, rather than falling asleep.

Children learn because it is essential for their survival.   As we get older we somehow lose that natural ability, so we need to create challenges which stimulate action.

How do we stimulate action?

Take on new challenges, mentally, physically, financially, whatever will make life worthwhile.

On the other hand, if you have had a busy life, you may need to just sit still and do nothing so you can hear any messages your unconscious is trying to send, which the noise of your world usually blocks.

Imagine your portrait today.
All your yesterdays, your intentions, forgetfulness, and choices not to act contribute to this picture.
Add to this, whatever has been handed to you without your consent at birth, and over the years from accidents and hurricanes beyond your control. This combination of events is now you.

Don't worry about your past. Don't worry about your future. It is up to you to consciously evolve with every thought, word and act. This makes your future.

However, there are also

UNCONSCIOUS FORCES,

which manifest their presence by sending us messages we need to decode.

Freud's self analysis brought to his attention the internal workings of our minds as seen through physical signs and symptoms. These signal that all is not as we pretend that it is.

This strong interconnection between mind, body, and spirit became apparent to Freud from his personal research and from observing his patients.   He showed how jokes, and slips of the tongue, eye, or foot, forgetting or losing things, can all be signals that something is moving just below the surface, which wants to be seen, or spoken.

Notice your own slips and mistakes.

Pay attention to what you do, or forget to do,

and what slips out in mysterious ways,

such as –

I have left the keys to my office at

work again.

I have tripped three times today.

I often call you by someone else's

name, lately.

I left the phone off the hook two days

in a row.

I repeatedly dream of being violent and in fights.

I forgot we were going out

I forgot my mother's birthday, again.

Is it really our anniversary?

You laugh when you hear these happening to others.   They are so familiar.

When you notice signals in yourself it's time to ask - whom and what are you avoiding ?

It is time to change something in your daily life.

Ignore these messages, and they will keep demanding your attention more forcefully each time.

How do you begin to question yourself ?

You begin to catch yourself by asking some straight and simple questions.

For example –

Are you where you want to be at this moment?

What is on your list every day that you never do?

When will you turn your derelict

dream house into a castle?

(maybe you never will - maybe it

doesn't matter)

Even with the easy questions you will come

up against **invisible barricades** which

you have built to avoid doing something.

They are **action inhibitors** that had a

function when you were growing up, but

once you see them they can come down.

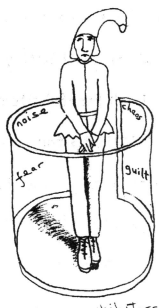

ACTION INHibiTors
are invisible barricades
you built to avoid doing
something - - - .

Fear is the biggest barrier, fear of -

authority, abandonment, failure, loss, the

dark, the darkness in yourself, and in your

imagined tomb.

To quell your fear you have set up a system, over the years, where you kid yourself and other people in all fearful situations. You create excuses for your action, or non action - yes but, I would have, I was going to, I didn't intend to. What would I do if - you left me, I lose my job, my looks?

Accepting your fear, loneliness, laziness, or disinterest, makes it easier to stop kidding yourself and adopt a more functional way of acting, or choosing not to act.

Embrace the human condition -
full of contradictions, foul
language, dirty deeds,
unsurpassed beauty, joy, and
ecstasy.

Another obstacle to creative action
is the burden of guilt that we each
inherit which inhibits your freedom
to act.

Guilt screams that you don't do enough, give enough love, time, or money to your parents, children, friends, or the world of polluted nature and starving people.

The only thing to do with guilt is to recognize its face, call it by name. Examine it. If there is no logical reason for that ache, then accept guilt as a part of you which is acting up, as your appendix might for no apparent reason. Check it out and then forget it.

Next, you will come up against
old verbal patterns,
which are defenses against action.

Phrases such as - I can't do it, I don't
want to, no I won't, were learned in
childhood and had a function to help you
become independent.   You also learned
responses, which were protection from
continual pressure from family and society to
get better grades, to earn more money, be
more physically attractive.

These niggling irritations and inhibitors often remain and are enough to keep you busily occupied, ignoring, denying, or forgetting, that most important element of confronting yourself.

How do you get rid of your many fears and see and accept your actions, as good enough?

To silence, or turn down, your ancient, internal voices and fear

learn to be less dependent on acceptance of your ideas from others.

Evaluate those authorities and experts who make superficial comments, voicing the consensus of those in power at the time. They will both criticize and flatter you with little understanding.
Judge the merits of any thought for yourself and then act on that.

You need time and persistence, plus information, in order to change anything in your life.
Take the time, develop persistence, the information is in your hands.

Now, give yourself some credit for
surviving this long in a complex
world.

Learning what you need to live a
flourishing life keeps you from
falling into an emotional pit.

Questioning is part of that
learning process.

As you question you will see that many of
your trouble spots have come from far back
in your past. Finding the roads which lead to
those wounds will release you from their
power.

The scars from past wounds show themselves as disturbing symptoms, such as *feeling anxious about your life most of the time, to forgetfulness, or sleep problems, and disturbing dreams.*

The PROCESS OF RENEWAL I am suggesting is like an astronaut's space walk to repair damaged parts on a satellite.

You concentrate - repair
what needs it, quickly – and
return to earth.

You don't remain in unprotected space going over and over things.
The point is to complete your journey and return.

Your
Self Analysis.

You are now involved in

SELF ANALYSIS,

a valid method of discovery.

It is not new.

Looking into yourself has been done by

philosophers for thousands of years in

different ways,

always to promote both insight and

action.

In the 16th century there was a famous

doctor, Paracelsus. He had a method of

analysing his dreams, and those of his

patients, which he used to find causes of

their symptoms.

By the late 19th century there was Freud
who spent years in self analysis.
Jung also delved into his unconscious,
through his dreams for several years, in a
process of self analysis.

However, by the 1920's psychoanalysis with
an analyst was considered the only method of
finding out about your self.
Self analysis, as a valid method was buried
for half a century.
Now, at the beginning of the 21st century,
developing the capacity for self analysis is
recognised as a goal of analysis, to be
learned by the client.

Joyfully I shout - **at last**.

Conquering territory through your
own initiative, courage, and
perseverance, gives you new
strength.

Self analysis is different from mere
self observation .
There is a synthesis of thoughts and
feelings, combined with your incentive,
your persistence, and
your deep need to feed your soul.

I want to give you

an astronaut's guide to repairing

your inner problems.

It will help you see the overall picture.

Here is a synopsis of a

method to get you started.

Before you settle down to contemplate in an

organized way

- prepare for your sessions.

HOW ?

First - arrange enough privacy, quiet, and time to relax, so that your mind settles. It takes a lot of practice and determination to understand what your unconscious is calling to your attention.

Second - create a method to review what you have done. You will go over and over certain more difficult areas as you progress.

You can review in several ways -

1 - **writing questions and answers in a journal** and going back to them to see if you have more answers at a later date. The benefit of reading again what you have written is that you will notice unexplored problems.

2 - **corresponding with someone** who is reliable, a holding place for your feelings and thoughts and who will keep them confidential.

3 - using a **tape recorder** to listen to your sessions.

4 - **painting** whatever you are feeling at the

moment.   Painting often encourages words

to follow.   Have the paints, or pens, and

paper handy.

You have prepared –

NOW BEGIN.

<u>To begin</u> - sit quietly and let your mind wander. Let your unconscious surface in whatever manner it chooses.

Focus your intention on understanding some hidden or undeveloped part which is swimming close to the surface of your awareness.

This is a fishing expedition to hook symbolic representations of your character, as well as memories.

Words, phrases, characters, or parts of your dreams, or incidents from your past may surface. Perseverance and time are essential. As images or words appear, let them unfold.

Any memory, recent or distant, that comes up is a gift for you to open and examine. Pay attention to your stories.

For example -

You may have a very clear image of going swimming in the river with your brother in the hot Texas sun and being offered cold watermelon by a Japanese man interned during the war in your town. You ran away because you were frightened of him, due to the newsreel pictures you had been seeing about the war.

Questions to ask yourself about any story or image-

1 - Why has this particular image come to your mind?

2 - How did you affect people and events?

3 – How did others in the scene affect what happened?

4 - How might you act in a similar situation now?

Ask the questions, then stand back and recognize your fears, prejudices, inexperience, hopes and dreams.

Go through this

process over and over

about the same issue

until you are clear

about it.

Look at what was done in the past and

say to yourself

I did not need that.

I needed . . . in order
to thrive.

I need . . . for a
flourishing life now.

This is cleansing questioning of yourself
and others, cutting through all the – yes-
but-replies.   Work toward that.

The point of this process is

- to gain a clear picture of

your part in every situation.

Combine this with the certainty that

what happened to you when you were

small and you had no say, was not

your fault.

Whoever took care of you may have

done their best, but it may not have

been right for you.

Clarify that. Remember it.

You are not responsible for what happened to you as a child but you are responsible for what you do with your life now.

This is a very important message for each of us.

This is not the time to approach others about what they did to you which you feel was damaging.   At a later time you can tell them -- or you may decide it no longer matters if they were wrong.

see   -- Suggested Reading -- Freud   Jung

Karen Horney   Alice Miller   Konrad

Stettbacher

What else will you

encounter on your quest ?

As you have begun to question yourself,

also look outward for people who

are healthy, lively, contented

with what they love doing, as

guides who can encourage you.

Notice what are they doing in their lives
that works for them.

Ask yourself and them
some searching questions.

FOR EXAMPLE –

What makes me feel life is good?

Who do I love?

Am I putting something of

value back into the world?

Why am I lonely?

What do I want to leave behind

when I die?

What am I not doing that I want

to do?

Do I live mainly on automatic pilot?

Why am I isolated?

Which essential parts of my life
are missing?

What part do I play in family
fights?

Why was she angry?

Get some answers from people and from yourself. You can always find someone, younger, or older than you who is creating something which inspires you.

You have the option of creating something of your own, of changing what can be changed in your daily life, if it matters enough.

Questioning your life is an ancient philosophical study that leads to well thought out action.

Alchemy

is another ancient study which metaphorically
turns base metal into fine gold bringing with
it the hope of treasure, which stimulates
action.

Hundreds of years ago alchemists
working together tried it in their
labs, as well as in their spiritual
quests.

Action analysis brings out the
alchemist in you.

This is an ongoing process giving you the space and the permission you have been denying yourself, to unite and transform your many facets into a richer, powerful new creation.

You turn unformed thoughts into considered words and then into rare and fine action.

As you question yourself you will begin to hear CLEARLY THE WORDS you use, or hear from others, which are only PRETENSE INSTEAD OF ACTION.

These are

Empty words

and are a problem for you and for the person

you are speaking to.

THEY ARE WORDS WITHOUT

SUBSTANCE.

Here are some other common ones.

Almost is one of those words to question,

because it can mislead you. You kid yourself

that you have already done something, when

you haven't. Are you almost persuaded ?

You can't almost do self analysis, almost

change, almost love your neighbor, almost give up smoking, drinking, hitting out, or almost win the pools.

You didn't. You haven't. You don't.

Almost but not quite, is like **nearly**. I nearly came to see you, translates, but I didn't. It sounds impressive and full of anticipation, but you say it to reassure yourself and anyone else who is listening that you have good intentions.

You don't do anyone a favour when your thinking is not precise.

> **For example -be precise, if you can.**
>
> Dinner is almost ready.
>
> *How long before it is?*
>
> Your car isn't ready.
>
> *When will it be?*
>
> I am almost ready to sign the contract.
>
> *When will you sign it?*

Empathy has become jargon and lost what impact it may once have had.   You imagine you understand someone's feelings.   You empathise with someone, feel good about your ability to be empathetic, and do absolutely nothing, a safe counselling technique.

However, EMPATHY is a mental process and not related to the more powerful words –

sympathy, or compassion - which call for you to do something to help.

Expectation is another obscure concept.   Expectations are formed by your childhood experiences.   As an infant you build up a picture of how your father and mother act, and react to you.   Then the picture enlarges to include other relationships and the community in childhood.

These expectations become internal pathways, effecting you consciously and

unconsciously, to which you return
regularly throughout life.   This inner
picture, built up over the years, forms your
unique stance toward encounters and
relationships. It becomes what you expect,
both good and bad, from people you meet
along the way and may stop you from seeing
the situation freshly and responding to the
moment.

A story comes to mind along these
lines of expectation, and conditioned
response.

There was a young student who anxiously climbed several thousand feet up to a small cabin where his teacher was staying. As he got nearer he saw smoke curling from the chimney, and his heart grew lighter for the rest of the climb.

When he arrived he met the teacher, who calmly welcomed him in, told him to make himself comfortable, and then went out again.

A while later he heard the teacher outside enthusiastically greeting a wandering dog who had come past the hut. The student was shaken and sad that his welcome had not seemed as warm.

We are left with the teacher's wise
response to his question -
*a puff of smoke makes the heart grow
lighter,   a kind word to a dog and the
heart grows sadder.*
Disappointment is a result of
unthinking, expectation.
As you become aware of your habitual
reactions, you can then respond creatively.

Experience is a confusing word.
It may mean you have lived a long time and
done things over and over, but it says nothing
about the quality of your understanding.

To say - *he is an experienced carpenter*
may mean he's constructed a lot of ugly,
faulty cabinets. It's another one of those
words often used to stop someone from
questioning, a so called, expert.

What has your experience taught you?

What do you know ?

Foresight is what you brag about when
you bought enough supplies to last through
the month you were snowbound. It also
enables you to castigate your lover for not
having enough wood in the storm. It is often
related to luck, not necessarily clever
planning.

You have drifted into the realm of magical thinking when you consider foresight to be something you possess.

Hindsight is a useless concept in action analysis. You did it, or you didn't do it. The results of that decision are yours to accept and transform as part of your creative life. Whether you were right or wrong is irrelevant, and in most circumstances difficult to assess, using hindsight.

A better method is to practise the very best creative thinking, consider every alternative, to try and avoid what you call a mistake, and then base your actions on these considerations.

Hindsight is only valuable to remind you to sharpen up your act now.

The idea that you possess hindsight gives birth to the equally useless - If Only...

which calls for -

BUT You Didn't, It Isn't, and WHAT NOW ?

If only... forms part of an imaginary thinking trap. What are you doing now to avoid saying it in the future?

Use lateral thinking, bring in the widest, most far-fetched possibilities.

Then, decide and act.

You really don't know what would have happened if only you, or someone else had done things differently.

INTENTION,

I intend to....

What are your intentions ?

We have all been asked these questions.

Kidding Yourself

I intend to be a tender lover, but
am I ?   Was I ?   Will I be ?
Your intention is your hope, or your
thought before you act.

I may intend to write in order to climb out of a low period, but until I do the writing, the intention is not transformed into action.

JUDGMENT - judgmental or non

judgmental are concepts which can cause you to have a tightness in the pit of your stomach. These words frighten each of us. You decide if your judgment is good, or if your judgments need more careful research. This is about releasing yourself from the hold of taboos, conditioning of all kinds which cloud your thinking, and make you fearful of deciding your own code of behaviour.

Turn off those nagging, judgmental,

voices in the courtyard of your mind,

stirring up emotion,

saying you're no good.

POTENTIAL is empty without action

turning it into substance.   Saying you are

potentially very talented can make you

think you are successful - without putting

in the effort, without the creation.

What you need is to produce - paintings,

actions, maybe even a productive gold

mine.

Regret is a meaningless word we hear and say too often. There must be corresponding action. **It means you are not now repeating the act you say you regret.** Fail to act, when it is right, and you start the cycle of regret again.

Sorry means you got caught doing or saying something your parents, society, or others disapprove of. When you are a child, adults try to make you be good, by their standards. We have all heard - all too often -

'Say sorry to the lady'

When you are a grown up, it is meaningless to say sorry, unless you have stepped on my foot, and don't intend to again.
If you feel sorry for someone, then ask them if you can be of some help.

Pause here

TACTICS FOR SURVIVAL

Practical applications and examples

We create tactics for survival. Some of them from childhood no longer fit our needs and are counterproductive. We learn as we go along from others and from stories and myths through time.

Here are some tactics that I have encountered.

Avoidance - means keeping away from - or preventing - something from happening.

Use the concept cleverly as a tool to avoid unwanted attention or emotions.

You may get it wrong, as in this **story** of the Fool who told his wife he wished to avoid seeing a certain man.

When the doorbell rang she said her husband was out. To which the man suggested she tell her husband, when he returned, that it was careless to leave his face hanging in the upstairs window while he was gone.

Use avoidance as a deliberate tactic by refusing to go down a road of blaming, anger, or hurt.

Ways to use avoidance as a tactic.

Avoid meeting that newly married ex.

Learn to say loud and clear to yourself, that <u>you will not go there</u>.

Avoid going places where you are not comfortable, spend too much money, drink too much, or don't enjoy the conversation.

Practise the art of choosing your own time to deal with emotions.

There are innumerable ways to avoid doing something, while at the same time kidding yourself that you are being productive.

Reading the computer manual from cover to cover, again and again, not actually producing anything on screen, is one way.

Once again, let's look at Nasrudin, the wise fool from many eastern tales who is our mirror.   He provides many examples of avoidance.   *Rather than admitting his own stingy nature, or his bad previous experience with his neighbour who had come to borrow a rope,   Nasrudin said it wasn't possible to loan it, because he had hung his flour on it to dry.*

What or who are you avoiding, or need to avoid ?

WHERE is the entrance to begin looking into myself?

This somewhat mystifying process of self analysis, of continually looking into yourself with a different mirror, can take you to any time in your life.   You can look randomly at parts of your life which seem to disturb you, or you may choose to begin from birth.

BEGINNING again - from the beginning.

This is related to looking back but the purpose in self analysis is to scan your childhood gently, and then return to look at the fruits of your life experience which make you who you are now.

What happened to you in the beginning of your life is only of interest because of the fruit it has born, and this includes traumas.

Scars are also fruit.

As the farmer who experiences
seasonal work knows, no one season
produce the reward.
Your childhood did not, of itself,
produce who you are.
There are many other elements in your
story.

Strange encounters, and people who
were unknown witnesses to your
struggles have each had some impact.
So, take a look, but come back and
continue here.

BACKWARD GAZE.
There is no future possible to see
ahead of you.

It is possible to get stuck in a

backward gaze.

This is a dangerous stance.

You can't go forward in that position.

The most important thing about the

past was that you lived it, with all the

emotions the living provoked.   None of

that exists now.

Going over and over what might have been

has no value.   Who you are now, as a

result, does.   So, take a swift look at any

old baggage, old clothes, which no longer

quite fit you, and pick up only what fits you.

Close the trunk, finally, and leave it behind

as a completed episode.

MEMORY is an ever changing

kaleidoscope.

Episodes from your past shift as

your viewpoint shifts with your

changing life experience.

The past is another country,

dangerous to become lost or

enchanted there.

It is not lovelier in that dim, distant past.

The new picture you are creating now is

the beautiful place to live.

NOTICING YOUR

SYMPTOMS

Your barometer, your unconscious, your psyche, or you soul if you prefer, may be shouting for your attention. Like any barometer you need to check it and see the forecast. Will there be clear skies or turbulence, wind, and storms?

If you are; sleeping badly, having disturbing dreams, feeling low more often

than ok, getting sick too often,
forgetting your keys,   calling people by
the wrong name,   tripping over paving
stones too often,   missing appointments,
feeling listless, lonely, bored, then stop
and listen.   The answer will come to
you, but you have to make enough
quiet each day to hear.

To find out where some
adjustment needs to be made
in your life, look at how you
work and **love.**

Ask questions,

then clarify and change what is unacceptable,

or accept it as who you choose to be.

For instance -

Are you working on a creative project

in some part of your life?

Are you just keeping busy - filling or

killing time?

Do you work -

to stay away from home

to feed yourself or your family

to be what your parents said you should
be

to gain status

to feel like a martyr

to feel powerful

to stop yourself from thinking or
feeling

because you can't think of anything
else to do

or work because you enjoy it

?

Ask yourself similar questions about

how you love, and treat your family

and friends.

Also

Do you give, and get, the kind of

attention you need to be content?

Although, if you are content, you probably won't ask why.

Don't ignore physical or emotional symptoms and sleep problems. They are your body shouting at you to pay attention.

Catching Yourself

in self delusion is a rewarding sport to learn in this process of self analysis.

Observe yourself carefully and notice your pretenses.

CATCHING YOURSELF IN
SELF DELUSION

I have **an example** of how I catch myself.

I say that I am going to India to find
enlightenment.   In reality, I am travelling,
and may be feeling special in my search for a
higher power, or feeling brave for going on
the adventure on my own.   As to
enlightenment,   I may not even be asking
the right questions.   However, if I am able
to recognise my self delusion, I will no longer
need to prove myself in a realm, which I may
not understand.   This frees me to enjoy
travelling, and to feel good about my courage
to take this journey.

Another example is creative work.

I have said, to myself, that I want to give ideas or art work to the world, freely.

But– Have I put it on the internet?

Is it possible that I want recognition, maybe even money, for these creations ?

How would I feel if someone else gets similar creative ideas out in the world before I do?

Each of us has complicated
motives for our actions.

It is an invaluable experience to take the
time to clarify motives, over and over,
because while they are hidden they effect
our behaviour in ways we may not see.

So, what do I control in

my life, if anything?

As I go through this process over and over I begin to spot what I need more of, and less of, to have a **flourishing life cycle.** This is the goal after all.

You have control over some areas of

your life some of the time.

Use them to your advantage.

Most of the important elements which we are handed in life, such as our family and inherited traits, or birth place and time in world history, do not come with the option of a choice.

Action analysis starts with

the premise that what you do,

most of the time,

is what you consider to be most

important for you to be doing,

at the time.

If you want to do something enough, or not

do something enough, you will find a way to

do it, or to avoid it, when the

circumstances are under your control.

For example –

It's no good saying, year after year -

I really want to be a taxi driver.

You aren't one.

I really want to live in Australia.

You have no plans.

You're kidding yourself.   You may need an
escape dream, a hope, a fantasy, for
awhile as inspiration.   But be clear in your
own mind what purpose your fantasy is
serving and move from dream to reality.

To make this move confront your automatic thinking patterns.

See the whole picture, which might include you as a taxi driver. You may be the doctor's daughter - Pete's sister, Tom's wife, Maria's mother, but you are much more as well. It is within your control and it is up to you to make your life complete. When you do this you also contribute to your chosen community with all the richness of your being.

To see the whole picture of who you are - carefully assess your skills and resources at any given time and then combine what is already around you, within your reach, to broaden the scope of who you are and what you do.

In this ancient story, Nasrudin, the eastern wise man and fool, who is often our guide, gave similar advice to a bored shopkeeper.

He suggested the shopkeeper could make boots to sell, by combining the leather, thread, nails, hammer, and glue, which were scattered on his shelves just gathering dust.

The shopkeeper had not stood back and seen all the possibilities.

Go back to your dream and make it real.

Learn to be the taxi driver.

Get behind a wheel.

Study maps.

If Australia interests you, go and get the visa papers from the embassy.

circumstances not within
your control.

These are circumstances you can control, remembering that there are always other elements which may enter the story as it evolves.

Let's look at the many circumstances not within your control.

Part of the beauty and pleasure of action analysis comes from forming creative, maybe even wild alternatives to what you are doing. However, there are inevitable changes that come with age, as well as unexplainable catastrophes, tragedies, and illnesses, which strike you.

When this happens you can only deal with the aftermath, as you would a meteor hit.

These changes are beyond your foresight, comprehension, or control.   They just happen.   Poverty, war, and illness may come along causing you to question what life means.

However, during these times of physical and emotional turmoil your survival instincts have to take priority.   Answers of a philosophical nature, as to meaning, have to wait until the turmoil settles.   Your challenge then is to combine the skills you have acquired over the years, to fit each new situation as it comes.

In these circumstances hindsight is of no benefit. Asking what you might have done only stops clear thinking and delays action.

Speaking of the natural, inevitable, course of life, there is a **story** from ancient time.

It tells of a king who one day commissioned all the artists in his kingdom to create something that would fit every occasion, happy or sad, as a reminder to him of their skills and his position.

After many attempts, a jeweler produced a ring for him.

Engraved inside were the words,

"This too shall pass".

Action Analysis is a continual process of asking yourself difficult and unusual questions.

Ask yourself what you regret not doing.

Don't live off the energy generated by regretting. Concentrate and eliminate regret. Most of the major forces of nature are not under our control, although we try to tame them for our comfort and survival.
We build fireplaces and ovens - to control fire, swimming pools, dams and bridges -to control water, wind tunnels and wind breaks - to control wind.

This is the most we can do, so far.

However, nature takes over and laughs at our attempts. **All we can do is prepare for our own reactions to what happens to us.** We can do this by imagination, by creating something similar to a rehearsal. We preplan, as in - a life boat drill, a defensive driving course, martial arts, first aid, or physical, emotional and spiritual fitness training of all kinds.

Prepare to react by knowing what is valuable in your life and what your fears are.

Experience will show you when you have missed something vital, as the professor discovered, too late in this **story**.

The professor was castigating the boatman for his ignorance of grammar and his incorrect speech. He said the boatman was wasting his life. through his ignorance of grammar and incorrect speech.

Suddenly, the boat began to sink and the professor found, to his dismay, that he could not swim. The one task he really needed to do before he got on the boat, he had neglected.

Have I done what I need to, up to today?

It is up to each of us to do what is necessary in each situation to finish it, and let it go.

You free your future, and prevent the build up of scars and symptoms by completing each episode during your day.

Completion also frees you from the burden of recurring hindsight and the old refrains, if only, or why didn't I ?   These voices inhibit moving on and solve nothing.   Close that chapter and begin a new one, not forgetting what you have learned.

An example of what completing an episode means is illustrated in the following **story**.

There were two monks, teacher and student, on a pilgrimage, when they came upon a lovely young woman at the edge of a stream, unable to cross. The older monk picked her up, carried her across, and set her down on the shore. Hours later on their walk the young monk said he was troubled by the teacher's action. They had been told not to touch women. The teacher replied that he had carried her across the stream and put her down on the shore. It appeared that the young monk was still carrying her.

He had not completed the episode.

It is essential for each of us to practise

Creative Thinking.

It shifts your perspectives to perceive in a
different way.   Change your perspective
and you change the situation and your
resulting actions.

For example, how I perceive a large
fish will depend on how close I am to it's
mouth, or whether I am a swimmer, a
fisherman, a photographer, or a marine
biologist.

From each of these perspectives the fish
will assume different proportions.
Feelings toward it of fear or scientific
interest or financial gain will also shift,
as well as whether I approach it with a
camera, a hook, or a stun gun.

Each story makes is obvious that we
are multifaceted, like a crystal with
many faces.
I am each of the characters at some time.
Big and small, light and dark, rich and poor,
good and evil, happy and sad, female and
male, old and young, greedy and generous,
are all aspects of each of us.

missing characters

Bring back the missing
part you left behind.

So, how do you bring all these characters together and accept that we are all the same at our core ?

As we grow up we learn to separate parts of us, to push them out as undesirable. We see, describe, assess and trap ourselves and the world in compartments, and then we ascribe what we don't like as belonging to others.

As I scan my past I see aspects of my character which, out of fear, were denied, hidden, or left behind as I grew up. I bring these aspects into my life by letting

each hidden or forgotten part slowly awaken
in dreams or in my behaviour.   It is vital for
me to include the dancing girl, and the child
who spoke happily to strangers, as well as
the little devil in myself, if I am to be
complete.

Those parts I see and envy, or fear, in other
people are **my shadow**, showing their
presence by making me irritable toward some
characteristics in a friend, similar to my own
weak or unpleasant ones. For example -
thoughts I have , or remarks that slip out,
about a friend - she only cares about, money,
clothes, sexual attention, fame.

She doesn't care about her husband, house, or kids.   These words need to be looked at carefully as indications of some underground current in myself.
I may not like someone because she is so bossy, so interfering, or critical.   Could any of these words have my name attached?

I mistakenly project all that I don't accept about myself onto others.
I give them my creativity and my anger to live out, and squander my birth right in this way.

I need to discover what is mine and patiently bring it back home. Without the full spectrum, from black to white, I am not whole.

Look at what is called the DARK SIDE of each of us. The one you hide which can be creative. Claiming it is one of the most valuable long term rewards of the work of self analysis.

Recognising the fundamental good and evil that you share with everyone else liberates you from guilt, shame and blame.

Jung called this dark side your personal shadow. You recognise it when you are honest. See your greed, your jealousy, and take responsibility for how you behave.

For instance, how much difference is there between taking cheap pens from the office and collaborating with, or at least befriending, opponents in a period of historical conflict? Maybe only circumstances.

There is also a kind of **collective madness** when a group or country goes desperately wrong, into extremes of prejudice and hatred.   This may be show itself in witch hunts, scapegoating, genocide, horrors of all types which 'others' commit.

However, you are less likely to fall into the more serious problem of this collective shadow once you have developed a deep understanding of what you and others are really capable of doing. You and I are just like those labeled different, sick, perverted, criminal, as well as those with different sexual or gender preferences, or differing religious beliefs.

Given the right kind of pressures and conditioning, as well as the right circumstances and price, you and I would be surprised at what we each might do to save a life, to surrender your life, or even perhaps to kill. When we deny our capability for the complicated feelings and actions of love and betrayal which exist together in us, we exclude the common humanity which we all share.

In **an example** from the Bible, Peter finally saw his capacity for duplicity when he heard himself denying that he knew Jesus, three times in one night, to save himself.

Peter and Judas both loved Jesus. They also suffered from fear, greed, and the desire for the power that they would wield, if only Jesus had declared himself King of the Jews when confronted by the soldiers in Gethsemane.

The story is complicated, as are the characters, and reminds each of us to look at our own hidden tendancies.   I must look at my fear, greed, envy, racist attitudes and my prejudices, not to wallow in how bad I am, or to be proud that I am the worst, but to **do something about them.**

Bring these hidden thoughts into the light and admit to yourself that you share them with other humans. You will feel less pressure to pretend to be someone you are not and be able to act and **react as you need to, not as you are told to.**

As well as observing your daily encounters, look for aspects of your nature symbolically portrayed in – myths, stories, the archetypes of Jung, goddesses, gods, icons and saints from many cultures. In each of these you will see the naked truth in one of her many disguises. As you stand back and see the full spectrum of your life you cannot fail to discover the obvious fact that there is some personal gain, creative outlet, or stabilising purpose in what you are saying and doing, even if it is keeping you in a familiar depressed state. These may be **hidden gains**, until you recognise them.

For example, you will leave an unsatisfying relationship, **finally,** when that last feather is put on the scale tipping it towards an intolerable state. The gain you have been getting, even in terrible circumstances, is finally outweighed by some minor gesture, and you will leave, even though it seemed unthinkable shortly before.

Nothing has changed externally to make it easier to leave, but you do. Be patient with yourself and learn to assess the right time for your action.

Another example can sometimes be seen in non specific depression, which is familiar to me. In this state I make myself inaccessible to others, I stay home as much as possible. Loved ones may be worried about me, and I haven't got the energy to face what is bothering me. I haven't the energy to be angry, to leave, to be hurt, to get a new career, or a new lover. Of course I haven't gone to get counselling, or pills.

However, I know this is a "prison" I have chosen, rather than some other form of escape and I will remain depressed until I make some move to get out of it.

It is also possible that this dark pit in my stomach will disappear, one day, just as suddenly as it arrived.

On the other hand, maintaining the patterns of your behaviour in your daily life may be necessary until you find a better way.

Even pretending to yourself can have a function, for a time.

There is wisdom in the saying -

Don't cut down the tree as long as it is giving shade.

However, when you get strong enough, you won't need to pretend.   You can develop other alternatives that are already on the horizon.

Once you have questioned and seen something, you can no longer not see it.

A useful **metaphor** for preparing yourself to face what ever comes in life is to develop the DISTANT VIEW of the CAMEL *NOT* the CLOSE VIEW of the DONKEY.

The camel sees into the distance as things draw near which gives it time to move and to react to what is coming. The smaller donkey sees mainly the ground in front of it on the road and the approaching lorry may be near too quickly for it to move out of its path. Like the donkey, you may not always pay attention or accurately judge the speed of the oncoming trouble. Sometimes you forget, and fall asleep when life is at stake.

Hopefully, you have prepared and learned to recognize warning signs sent to you from various signals in your body. You will also need friends or guides who will give you a hand when you forget to be vigilant.

We have **the example** in this story of **the king's son.**

The boy was sent to earth as part of his training for kingship.

His task was to find a treasure, guarded by a huge dragon.

However, he got distracted from his mission by all the bounties on earth and exhausted, fell into a deep sleep.

This had been foreseen as a possibility by
the wise teacher who had sent him.
A familiar and beautiful sound, unique to
his planet, was sent to awaken him.
Hearing it reminded him of his quest to
retrieve the jewel and return home.
Each of us faces inevitable distractions that
make us forget what we are doing.
However, our developed intuition and
vigilance can warn us of danger.   Observe
yourself, avoiding a state of - if only I had
seen it coming,
I could have ....

Dreams are another tool for

understanding yourself, given as a gift

during sleep.

Dreams are calling you to notice, to be aware

of something, and to act on the message.

We have analysed dreams since someone first

said - I had a funny dream last night.

Which ever method you choose to analyse

yours, the important meaning is one you

understand.   An interpretation given by

someone else is meaningless without your

resounding yes .

147

How you see each segment, each character, as a part of yourself or your community depends on how your culture values or dismisses dreams. Dreams may be Freudian or Jungian in style, if you have analyst of either persuasion.

You may see dreams as reformatting or cleaning up your mental desktop after a difficult day or time. You may see them as foretelling your future, or messages from dead loved ones. You may have a series of dreams that only make sense to you as you see things repeating in each one.

As with your waking creations, search for clarity and appreciation of what this dialogue you are having with yourself is trying to tell you, and then decide where to go with it, how to see it.

A different kind of dream are the fantasies we keep in a

DREAM Cabinet.

We create a place in our brain full of files labeled – intentions, hopes, and self delusions, which we keep as secrets.

Observe what you store and why you keep it.

For instance, it provides a temporary place of safety for embryonic creations, ideas, or projects you are working toward which need a safe place to grow before they face the inevitable storms of criticism.   Providing a safe space is a valuable function, but you need to return to this cabinet often to see if ideas are developing or if they should be thrown out.

On the other hand, like every hiding

place, it has a dark side.

You can be drawn here when you are low,

to beat yourself up for what you might

have done, but didn't.

For example,

I have been thinking and talking about

returning to Greece to live ever since I left

thirty years ago, without any action to go.

Relevant questions

to ask myself are -

-why have I hung onto this dream,

-what is it doing for me now as a

fantasy .

During this time I have lived in several countries, with a good deal of difficulty, legally, financially, and emotionally, while believing I intended to return to Greece. I have always had the option of going to Greece. Instead, I have lived with the emotion stirred up by thinking that, like Marlon Brando, I could have been a contender for the championship, rather than facing the reality of action, of fighting in the ring and risking failure.

However, I no longer need to stir up emotion in this way, or to beat myself up, because this is what I have been doing all this time.

I choose to put down roots here, where I have obviously chosen to live - because I am here.   This fantasy no longer has a purpose and I can go to my dream cabinet and throw it out leaving space for storing new, more creative, ideas.

Along the lines of releasing

ourselves from dreams, or

demons we don't want, so that

new things can grow,

an ancient story

shows us how.

DURGA, Hindu, fierce,

compassionate *Goddess was called to*

come and save the world just as demonic

forces were about to destroy it .

She entered the battle with a roar,

killing wave after wave of demons as they

came back in different disguises .

She never gave up.

From time to time a sigh would escape her lips, and other feminine warriors would spring up and help her in the battle.

Eventually, the last and most terrible Buffalo demon came at her.

They battled fiercely.

She cut off his head, and he rolled from the scene.

However, the chief demon was watching the battle.

Infuriated by the defeat of his forces, he determined to kill Durga himself.

First, he tried to seduce her, but she
fought of his powerful forces.
Then he challenged her to meet him alone
on the battle field .

She agreed, and after intense, close
combat, rolling around the heavens
intertwined, she managed to draw her
dagger and pierce his heart.

His body tumbled from
the universe, leaving the earth once more
safe.
Durga did not stay to rule the
world, but promised to be there if called.

Durga's enduring power is within you and me, if we summon it.

But what does that mean?

Intellect and rational are not enough in this inner conflict. I intend to do something, or to stop doing something. My mind is made up that I will change. Intellectually I am certain that I am in control of myself, that I cannot be seduced by power, money, or lust. However, there is more required of me. Only when my heart is pierced, when it is touched, when I have reached the heart of the matter is the battle really over.

I am free when my heart

is laid open and from it

the flower of change grows.

Some of our most distressing **emotional**

states seem to be unexplainable.   They

can come on you for no apparent reason.

These states are not to be confused with

passions or emotions as a result of tragedy.

All you can do at the time is to acknowledge your agitation and remember that you are free to move away from it, or stand back and observe until it passes.

For instance, I am longing for someone, or something, and realise that what I am experiencing is a state of non specific longing, of agitation. Whatever object I find right then to hook my emotion onto will provide a temporary release - a film, an ice cream, or maybe a stranger. There are times when I recognise this state I am in and let go of my anxiety or emotion by stepping away and saying - NO, take another path.

Other times, when I am agitated, I will yell at my companion, or child, or animal.

Then there are other times when I can't do anything, but remain in the emotional state until movement is possible as a result of some new element becoming conscious and clarifying what is bubbling underground.

An example of this state comes from Liz, who is in this state of uncertain agitation, a funny feeling in the pit of her stomach. After some consideration she comes up with the idea that it is to do with her lover.

Their relationship is in a state of flux, nothing is certain about feelings on either part, but she doesn't want to leave - yet. She thinks about it, argues with herself, and finally decides she can now put up with the feeling having clarified this much for herself. The effort, time, and persistence she has taken to understand how she feels is well worth it.

Sometimes agitation is a flag from your unconscious trying to get your attention, telling you a message is on its way. Just be patient and wait for the message to become clear.

There is also the fact that, given enough time, some things resolve themselves.

Learn to leave it alone.

Restrain yourself from digging, or interfering, as this story will show.

Nasrudin was in court one day when the king was ranting.

The king wanted something to entertain him, immediately, or he would cut off all their heads.

Nasrudin said he had an idea.

He would teach a donkey to speak, with

the proviso that he was given ten years in

which to do it.

The king agreed, but swore to cut off his

head if he failed.

The courtiers were horrified, and said

that surely immediate death would be

preferable to ten years of waiting.

Nasrudin, however, whispered to them

that he was 75 years old, and the king

was 80.

In ten years time other elements would

have entered the story.

Another way to check out your emotional state is to review how anxious and preoccupied you are about the world, the neighbourhood, your family, and your health.

Ask yourself these questions.

Am I wallowing

in a state of anxiety ?

Am I generating emotion

because I lack it ?

Does my anxiety solve anything ?

Am I doing anything
to resolve my anxiety ?

Some states return again and again, like a
kind of recurring indigestion, as a reminder
that you haven't solved them yet.   They
require more action and more time, like a
prescription that doesn't cure your
symptoms over night.   **An example** is
anxiety, tightness, in your stomach because
you have stopped smoking, or drinking, or
seeing a lover.   This will lessen with time.

There is also a useful, mild, anxiety, for which there is no explanation. It is a pressure in your stomach pushing you to consciously evolve, to expand your alternatives, over and over throughout life. This anxiety is so common we forget its force on our moods and behaviour. Use its positive side to expand your life.

There are also **strong emotions** that trigger anger, hatred, jealousy, revenge, murder and war.

The Pool of Passion.

This dangerous area is the pool of passion - Avoid it.

What is this pool, and how do you and I stay out of it?

Which passions do I need to curb ? In this very difficult struggle to prevent the more dangerous emotions, begin with those of **anger** and **jealousy,** which call forth **revenge** and sometimes **war.**

The ancient fight in Troy over the beautiful Helen vividly portrayed the tragic consequences of unleashing emotions.   In every case it has to be prevention.   You do not have to respond with uncontrolled emotion.

It is not necessary, it is

counterproductive,

and it is destructive, always.

How do I avoid the pool ?

Do not go down the road that

leads to it in the first place.

At the first hint of jealousy shout at yourself - LOOK OUT, go another way, take the scenic route!

Once you slip into the warmth of the pool of passion, it is too late to control of the range of emotions which may surface.

If you have not stopped yourself, and get angry and jealous, then it is up to you to contain your emotions. It is up to you to protect others from any damage as a result.

It is a lie, one we politely call denial, to claim you can't control your emotions.

Hard as it may be, you always have the option of walking away from someone who maliciously, or unconsciously, pushes you into the pool.

However, it is vital for you to prepare in advance for your reaction to overwhelming passion, just as you educate and exercise the rest of your body and responses when you are trying to be fit.

My argument is that belief structures emotions and how we act on them.

Consider this.

I inherit the capacity to feel and exhibit several emotions in common with all humanity. How I choose to react to their signals depends on my moment in history.

For example, if I have been taught that when someone offends me I must physically fight her or him, then my feelings will be strong enough to do this.

However, we no longer duel over being bumped in the street, as a matter of honour, although it might produce a violent argument if I feel wronged or insulted.

Is this issue worth my anger?

If I feel that what has happened is of no consequence, I will not feel the emotion of anger, only slight irritation. This is also true for feelings of loss and grief. The strength of my feeling will be related to how valuable I consider the object, job, or person was for my well being and my place within my community, as well as my cultural and religious conditioning.

Expression of my passions are influenced or controlled by what I learn from my family and culture, including religious beliefs.

For instance, I may understand love with the same belief and value placed on it by my surrounding group, or rebel against it. If my culture has the belief that this passion we call love is worthy, then it may be easier for me to fall in love, and probable that I will open myself to all the other passions of anger, grief, jealousy, and more because that is acceptable in my group.

Are these worthy passions for me to fall into?

Can these be curbed ?

Should they be curbed ?

It is probable that belief as well as gene predisposition, structure emotions.

You can re educate yourself to curb your responses, always remembering the strength of cultural pressures to conform. You also need to work consciously toward further evolution of your ancient brain that may urge you to grab what you want.

You can recognise, and curb, the strong, natural drive to preserve the species. From this drive the concepts of possession, territory and war have developed. Unconscious triggers, such as, she is my lover and gene transmitter, or, he is my boyfriend and protector of my nest, overpower good sense when you feel threatened.

At that time, you must pull back and look at the wider picture. Ask yourself what you are doing to yourself, your loved ones, and your community when you actions are based on uncontrolled passion alone.

What can you change in yourself
that has been embedded by your
culture ?

What may be left over from an earlier
evolutionary development that is no longer
necessary for survival in the 21st century?

This is vital preparation for a time you
may be swamped and not thinking clearly.
Remember there are other scenic routes.
Avoid the pool and keep a friend
handy to pull you out in case you slip.

Let's look at a specific MOOD,

mild depression, which you may

Shift THROUGH ACTION.

It is certain that when the

discomfort is greater than the gain

of staying in any familiar territory,

I will move, one way or the other.

This describes all moods.

We each chose our particular mood prison.

You and I have to create the necessity

to get out of it,

if we want to enough.

You can learn to do this, most of the time.

Mild depression may come and go or last several weeks or months. It can also come, stay, and then disappear for no apparent reason. There is so much about personal chemistry and other factors contributing to depression that is not known.

Any attempt to release myself from depression takes advance preparation and the certainty that I do, sometimes, get in this mood and that I can shift it. Looking into myself during such a low period, I realise that deep in the centre of my being lies a certainty that I do not want to die yet.

In this dark place the realisation is positive and jolts me.   This is what I hold on to and from where I can pull myself up, or at least hold on.

I may be able, at this point, to consciously act, perhaps force myself to move, in some way that will get me on an upward slope. This may take several attempts and longer than others can understand.   This is a pit you have to have experienced to understand.

Perseverance definitely furthers.

But prevention is crucial.

This gloomy, and all too common, picture reminds me to stand back and observe myself, when I am feeling more energy once again.   Only at this point will I have strength to continue questioning myself, remembering that I am responsible.

What am I doing when I am low ?

Am I wallowing in this low place ?

Can I get out of it ?

Do I want to ?

Is it a comfortable, well known, space to be in ?

What am I getting
from staying in it ?

What, specifically, is done for me
when I am too depressed to do it
myself?

What am I avoiding during this
period ?

What effect is it having on my loved

ones ?

What can I bring into my life that I

am missing instead of getting

depressed ?

I try to understand myself and my

surrounding, and I still get

depressed.

Why ?

Does this mean there are unknown
factors and I just have to live
with these bouts ?

After considering and answering each of
these questions, what else can I
actually do to ease or eliminate
depression ?

I can begin by admitting to myself, and
others, that I am low and need a friend
or guide to talk to.   I am confronting
troubling questions of body and soul.

Another valid choice I may have to consider, is the possibility of taking the appropriate pills to lift my spirits and energy enough to be able to focus on the hope which will keep me going.

Recognising my responsibility for getting out of this jail I have put myself into frees me to give all my concentration to locating and preparing my release.

Each step, each action, comes from within me, or there is no movement at all.

My climb out this dark pit is solo, although I will gain energy and encouragement through sharing my path of errors and successes with loved ones, and from the kindness of strangers. I created my particular kind of prison, and this is the path out of it.

MOURNING

is another important time for each of us, for which we are often unprepared.

We mourn the death of those we love and, on a different level, the break up of relationships, loss of homes, jobs, and of course animals we have shared our lives with.

In our western culture we often deny death and loss, just as we deny depression, fear, and any personal pain or financial problems.

We often find ourselves unprepared for death.

We do not have personal beliefs, understanding guides,

or meaningful rituals to carry us

through these endings,

which are also new beginnings.

We spend more time planning meals,

holidays, and cleaning, than

contemplating, what is for each of

us, the most important coming event

we will experience.

It is a vital part of my life to prepare, to

come to some understanding of what may

have been before conception, of life and

death, and what may follow.

What my belief is will depend on my culture, my immediate family, education, personality, and what life experience has brought to my attention.

It only matters that I have a belief, not which belief will sustain me, at the death of my loved ones, and eliminate the fear of my own death. On a practical basis, mourning can be a process of creating new life from treasure left to us. You collect the memories, unfinished plans and actions from the past, make them alive for you in the present, and mould them into new life forms which will sustain you.

To do this you need to release your attachment to the past that stifles new life.

Bring back any personal treasure which you have given away, which they may, or may not, have wanted, or even realised they were carrying for you.

How have you given personal treasure away?

- when you give someone your choices to make for you, even simple ones about daily routines,

- when you do not take all your own rightful responsibilities for things you are capable of doing,

- when you live your life through the creations of a loved one,

- when you don't put yourself on the line by creating something of your own,

- when you expect your child to fulfill your hopes and dreams,

- when you live a dependent life,

- when you squander your resources
by leaving them dormant, and
undeveloped,

- when you do not know how to thrive
on your own.

You free your future as you bring back
these treasures, bring new skills into
your life and develop them creatively.

You may need skills now that you never
learned . These can be as elementary as
paying bills, changing fuses, or cooking.

Time, and these newly found abilities and interests, will give you strength to live with the fact of the separation from a loved person, or position.

This is not a smooth or painless path to walk.
It may seem like a path of crushed flowers, not new life.

You will swing back and forth between being OK, and then suddenly swamped by memories and emotion.
You won't forget, but you will not always wander, lost, in the past.

We are reminded of how to retrieve treasure through **stories,** where the hero has to develop hidden parts of himself. He must find ways to reach inaccessible mountain tops, fight demons and dragons in order to rescue the treasure which is necessary to save himself, a maiden, or a kingdom. Through these trials we can see the development of his, or her character.

This **story** of a dying man who had three lazy sons portrays this transformation, through seeking treasure in a very down to earth way.

An old farmer called his sons to his bedside and told them he was leaving them a treasure for their inheritance. It was buried in the fields. The boys were very lazy, but also very greedy, so they decided to try to recover the treasure. Field by field they plowed every inch. After many weeks they had found nothing.

However, as they had worked so hard, for the first time in their lives, and because it was the season, they decided they might as well plant. Then they sat back and watched things grow, as well as doing some weeding and watering.

When harvest time came they decided to bring it in, because they could then begin to dig again. They still had a treasure to find. They had a good crop, and made some money, which was a bonus.

Once again the cycle began. They plowed deeper and more carefully, because they felt sure to find the treasure this time, and so it went, season after season until they became strong.

Eventually it dawned on them how wise their father had been. He had left them a treasure, and they had found the true

path to enlightenment, as he hoped,

through working the fields, over and over

and over.

Like these sons, what you have been left will
change and grow through your simple,
creative actions year after year as part of
the cycle of continual renewal.

I want to widen this discussion of passion,
emotion, mourning, depression, and what
we can do to heal ourselves, to include

self healing on a community level.

Begin by looking at your personal shadow, an unrecognized side. It is through this unreconized part of yourself that you may fall into the larger, collective, shadow of a group in times of extreme emotional turmoil and mass hysteria in society.

This can arise quickly when individuals in any society have not looked at their personal shadow, their hidden, unexplored side. We often blame others, out there, for problems, beliefs, issues of any kind when we feel under threat of attack. We have each witnessed this process of blaming and attack too many times, all over the world.

How can we stop this blaming in the community and heal wounds already caused by internal fighting, hatred, and revenge?

The theory

is that when I accept my own dark, dangerous, potential, I can then bring personal projections back home, with an open heart, and not blame others for what is mine.

This can be done by a whole community and by groups as well.

There is a brave example from South Africa.

The process South Africa has devised involves a convicted criminal admitting guilt for his crimes in a special court, the Truth Commission.   The person claims that the crime was committed only because of the political situation at the time of the crime. He, or she, can ask to confront their victims - if victims are willing. The convicted person is required to tell their truth about what they did, and explain details of their actions.

They can then ask for forgiveness from the victims, or families of victims, although they may not receive this forgiveness, depending on their crimes and the family's response.

It is a complex process and radical idea which opens the door, allowing understanding to come back into the collective, psyche, mind, and vision.

This is a courageous effort to heal the disastrous splits between good and evil, us and them, black and white.
If it can be done, then they may avoid carrying over ancient feuds into future generations.

You take part in the same healing search for unity when you look at your life.

You break the pattern of passing on your family feuds, prejudice, ignorance and fear to future generations, as you surely do if you do not face the darkness in your heart, and change.

As a model of what is essential to sustain life, look at nature and the universe.
It is clear that day and night, sunlight and moonlight, have equal importance in generating life.

We are the children of nature, and we need both the darkness of deep red earth, as well as sun and starlight, to thrive and be completely human.

How does this understanding of nature fit in with the challenge I have undertaken to cope with the richness and turmoil of a complex modern life? Because, knowing that nature is forever changing helps me to concentrate on this moment.

This only happens with attention and practice.

Forgetting the moment causes me to lose my grip on the present, my focus on my actions, and messes up my future.
However, sometimes I become exhausted and distracted,
as did the woman in this

story.

A woman, on her way to market with a large jar of honey began to plan what she would do with the money when she sold the honey.

She would buy chickens, sell their eggs, and buy a cow.

Her fantasy continued..

Getting so excited over her future
wealth, she lost control of her present
hold on the jar of honey and had to
watch helplessly as the honey poured
onto the road.

She failed to realize her present
was her future as well.

Observing the gaps between

what you say and what you

do.

This is part of noticing and accepting your dark and light sides and changing what you need to.   You will be come experienced in this as you do it over and over.

For instance, I have been saying I

would walk every day in the park, but I have only been twice this week.   I said I would go and see my friend on Monday, but I didn't. I said I would stop smoking, stop seeing that man, stop drinking a bottle of wine a night.... Seeing this gaping hole between my intention and my action I realize all is not as I have been telling myself and the world that it is.

This can be a scary discovery.

BUT

Exploring this gap brings tremendous relief, as I recognize and accept where my heart really is.

This is a search for clarity and understanding of what I am doing, or choosing not to do, and there are no value judgments in the process. It is about eliminating the gaps between words and actions

There is a **story** that illustrates this process.

GOING TO DO

was a very special elf.

This is his tale, with a moral.

Going To Do could be found and heard every day, outside a cafe, speaking to admiring elves about what he was going to do.   First, he would get very healthy, and climb the tallest mountain.   Then, he would make a huge range of elfin toys to sell in his shop, and get very wealthy.   He would also learn all about the mysteries and art of sewing and make toy clothes, to which he would apply his personal hand painted designs.

The final touch would be unique hats he would design and sell in his workshop. Month after month he enchanted the elves with his plans, which they shared and accomplished, in their own minds, with him.

One day a visitor came from a far off mountain, sat down and listened to his stories.   She was captivated, and begged to be allowed to see his amazing workshop and learn his many skills.   He politely told her his place was too much of a mess at the moment, and quickly made his escape.

Suddenly, he was quite sick with the realisation that there was nothing for the elves to see, no skills to learn. All he had ever done was talk .

This could have been the end of the story, but in this case, all the elves realised they had also conspired to listen, not to ask questions, not to get involved, just to imagine and share in the glory. So, perhaps, they got together, and turned their words into substance.

But that's another story.

Going to do !

Stories and myths, with the heroines and heroes they portray, are an essential way to see, symbolically, who we are, what we are doing, and what each of us is missing in our character. From the beginning of oral, and later written, history there are characters, often paired in the story, who each needed the other to be complete.

For instance - Adam and Eve, Cain and Abel, Jacob and Esau, Moses and Aaron, Mary and Martha, Romeo and Juliet, Don Quixote and Sancho Panza,

Tristan and Isolda, Lancelot and Guinevere to Beauty and the Beast, complete the plot together, often metaphorically. In these stories the hero's search involves confronting some powerful force, which pushes his, or her, development through heroic deeds and misdeeds, as she risks life and limb, with the outcome uncertain until the very end.

The plot involves the metaphorical search for hidden or guarded treasure, or person, to rescue. Once rescued the treasure, or person, must be returned to the right kingdom. This is usually a difficult task and not always accomplished. You can see aspects of yourself in them.

During the sequences of the story the
heroine, or hero, has gone through extreme
exertion and trials necessary to reach
another spiritual plane and in order to gain
the treasure.   Then comes the important
and difficult process of bringing back the
treasure for himself and others. This
suggests the need to return to earthly values
and time, as well as living in the knowledge of
what has been experienced.

In some stories the hero is allowed to tell of
what he has experienced, in others it is
forbidden to disclose what he has seen.
Sometimes experience must be secret
because it would be misunderstood if not

seen first hand. He will remember his journey but must live out his life in the earthly plane while remaining aware that there is something else, some other reality, some other way of seeing.
Others will only vaguely sense a difference in him, something more solid, since his adventure.

You and I become totally caught up in these stories, and ancient myths. They mirror our struggles, defeats and victories against strong internal and external forces.

This identification is an unconscious attempt at self healing, understanding, and growth.

Daring to risk everything in this valiant search for what you are missing is part of action analysis.

In the **tale of Ulysses,** *he sailed safely past the enchanting songs of the sirens when every other boat had been dashed on the rocks.*

He plugged the ears of the oarsmen and tied himself to the mast.

He had to hear their alluring songs, but not surrender to the madness produced by the experience.

He was the character who went to a different plane, dared to gain knowledge, and came back changed in some way.

Each character, each image of a Goddess or a God, is a mirror reflecting some aspect of us.

For instance,

we see Zeus eating his child, killing for spite, and being kind out of a whim.

Like him, we are full of contradictions.

Myths help us to cope with our overpowering emotions, and to see our human frailties in a grander perspective.
Look into these myths for yourself.
Create your own personal myth, a story for your time.

In self analysis **I use stories** to unravel the riddle of how my mind works, and to question and resolve why I am so often bumping along the road instead of flying high in my daily life.

Metaphor, allegory and humour, in plays and myths help me to see aspects of my common humanity, the frailties,

joys, and sorrows we all share.

Stories help you and me to see the myriad

ways we kid ourselves.

Stories bypass internal censors and help

you to outwit yourself, as you glimpse

what you are really doing, and where you

are really going.

An ancient saying describes this insight

clearly for me.

You say you're headed for Mecca ?

I fear, oh pilgrim, that you are on the

road to Samarkand.

Stories also point out our misplaced faith in what we are told by authorities of all kinds.

Nasrudin, often our guide, is a famous character from Eastern tales.

He is a fool who is not a fool.

He is a beacon aiming point blank at our mad stances, which we see as quite normal.

See him, and you see yourself.

For example, in this story Nasrudin highlights the falsity of our belief in what we hear from men in white coats, those experts who would try to tell us where we go wrong.

These experts are too often totally
inexperienced in perceiving life for
themselves.

*One day Nasrudin decided to find out how
some scientists understand the nature of
things.   He proposed a test.   He asked
them to write down the definition of
bread.   They were unable to come
anywhere near a decision, which was, of
course, his point.*

We only have to look at the daily newspapers
to see these same follies and real life
contemporary dramas of world leaders,

experts of all kinds, laid out before us in black and white. It's worth a close look. Then ask yourself, how might you, or I, or Nasrudin, act in modern versions of ancient stories ?   Would we be brave or ignorant ?

How do you know if your action is inappropriate?

One way is to check and see if your action is having unexpected results. If so, then you probably haven't asked the right questions before you acted.   This is illustrated in this **story** of men who didn't think about the consequences of giving life.

Three men on a journey were very excited to find the complete skeleton of a tiger lying in their path.

One man had studied anatomy, so he managed to arrange the bones exactly as they had been when the tiger was alive.

The second man practised internal medicine, so he knew how to arrange the organs and give the kiss of life in order to restore breath to the tiger.

The third man told them they didn't'
know what they were doing, and being
a tree surgeon he, appropriately,
climbed to the top of the tallest tree.
He then watched sadly as the tiger
came to life and bounded toward his
recreators, who provided his first meal
in a long time.

JESUS also gave examples that clarify
appropriate action.   He clarified the
thinking and action of each person who
approached him.

To a rich young man, who asked him what he needed to do in order to be saved, he spoke in active terms. He told him to - come, give, sell, follow him. To disciples and others he said to cast their nets, or to arise. He also advised people to do nothing when that was appropriate, as when he said to consider the lilies of the field who do no toiling, but are of great beauty and value.

Jesus also cautioned you and me to consider our own dark side before casting a stone in condemnation of another person.

If the rich young man had been interested in self analysis, he might have seen that he was kidding himself when he approached Jesus. In a way that is all too familiar to me, he really only wanted to hear the sound of his own words, to feel good, not to act.

How often do I mistake my words for action ?

When I describe the house I am going to build, I see it as done.

Repeated promises that I intend to keep, but don't, delaying tactics, and excuses of all kinds, mostly beginning with - **but** - are all indications that I am not facing what I am really thinking, feeling, and wanting.

How often am I able to be as the lilies of the

field and openly display my nature to the

world, with no justification other than

I am ?

As well as appropriate and inappropriate

action there is the possibility of

choosing not to act.

Choosing not to act is a valuable concept,

which our family and friends will appreciate.

I choose not to give advice to my

friend, this time.

I choose to be quiet and let my child learn for her self, on this occasion.

I choose to walk away from   angry words, because it feels right.

I choose not to go down the road of all consuming jealousy, this time.

What is a necessary action in one situation, is not required in another.

This is the skill of being appropriately inconsistent,

and related to the phrase – this time.

You are not unconsciously avoiding

something.

You have chosen not to act.

In another case you may have trouble

making any decision.

However, in this state of indecision you have

a lot of undirected energy racing around in

you causing irritation, distress, exhaustion,

and sometimes pain in some weak part of your

body.   Catch this process before it goes

on too long.

When a decision is difficult to make, ask yourself

WHY ?

Look at decisions that are easy to make, and ask your self

WHY ?

Some **examples** of difficult decisions are –

-pressure from family to go to a particular school, or study a subject you don't want to,

-your boss may try to pressure you into taking a job you don't want,

-

-your partner may want a new car, house, kitchen, or set of golf clubs,

-your mother may want you to come to lunch twice a week.

Deciding what to do may be easier

when you remove –

fear of what someone else thinks,

greed on your part, and

lust for unnecessary power.

Remember that ENOUGH is the

crucial concept in research or

ambition, as well as in greed and

desire.

In all of your choices and your decision

making there is a complex interconnection

between the past and who you are and what

you do now.

How do interconnections show up ?
During self analysis try to understand the scars and the rewards from your past. Look for their origins, how you got them, as a way of understanding interconnections. However, remind yourself each time you look back at a series of memories that they are not factual representations of events .

Memories are painted with different tones depending on your perspective at that moment, and they change and fade with time.

You never put memories back exactly as they happened.

They are altered with each viewing.

Connections in stories, as in life, are often complex.

Nasrudin experienced these interwoven connections in a **story**, we are told.

He was walking along one evening and was frightened by the sound of hoof beats coming toward him.

In his terror he jumped over a wall and landed in an open grave.

The riders came along and stopped to ask why he was there, and if they could help him.

He replied that just because they could ask a question did not mean there was a simple answer to it.

The answer depended on one's viewpoint.

He said he was actually there because of them, and they were there because of him.

Everything is interconnected, but not necessarily in a clear-cut way.

The **story of Fatima** illustrates how to combine skills, to make connections, from the past into new creations needed now.

Fatima experienced many tragedies and upheavals, torn from one home and job to another country, repeatedly.

Eventually, washed up on the shore of yet another land, she was called upon to combine all of her skills and past experiences.

Over the years she had learned weaving, boat building, and rope making.

237

These were now the skills required to produce a tent for a king who had never seen one, but had dreamed of what one might be like.

She was able to assure her future because she had turned her trials and tribulations into expert skills that she combined in a way she could never have for seen.

Fatima is a model for you and me.   She did not fall into an emotional memory swamp, but saw interconnections in a situation where no one else had her skills or vision.

She was in tune with the RHYTHMS of the UNIVERSE, as you can be. Your entire life runs in sympathetic harmony with these rhythms. They are within each of us. Sense them in your breathing, your heart beats, your monthly cycles, your feelings with each changing season.

When you are in tune with your own rhythms, and supporting the rhythms of the society in which you live, you are also supporting the universal rhythm. These rhythms are all interconnected. They are the natural ebbs and flows of the need and desire for social gatherings and rituals, which celebrate the flow of nature and maintain unity in the family and community during the year. Historical time and cultural shifts affect how they are manifest. In Europe and North America autumnal festivals of Thanksgiving feel just right when you are in touch with the cycles of planting and harvesting. But, for others who have moved to a part of the world with opposite seasons an important yearly outdoor celebration may fall in mid-winter, instead of high summer, which makes adaptation to nature crucial. You get out of tune when you block out, ignore, or forget that you are part of the same rhythmical system as the rising and setting sun, moon, and stars.

It is easy to miss these events in our busy daily lives with cloudy and polluted city skies, so take a holiday where you can see the earth and the sky, and remember peace is in the emptiness.

Another important aspect of your daily life to consider is - how much attention, love, friendship, and work with others you need to keep you looking forward to another day.

-Do you have too much attention?

-Are you becoming isolated through ignorance of the consequences of lack of attention to your needs, in your busy, consumer oriented economies?

These are vital questions for your wellbeing. Do not ignore what you observe. As we have become more technically able within our culture we are also tending toward more personal isolation.

Instead of houses full of people, we fill them with mechanical devices which we rely on.

242

I can kid myself someone is there when I turn on Elva, my computer, with her silver screen and bright greeting.   She has light, a voice, and communicates, but is not alive.   I can turn on the radio or television and hear and see people.

However, I also need to give and get enough attention from people, in order to thrive.   Machines do not provide this. I long for connection, and when I am feeling disconnected from loving people I also feel physical, emotional, and spiritual malaise and pain.

I now recognise these symptoms, and act in a self healing way to repair the damage that I have caused myself. I also prevent continuing damage in the future by understanding what I really need to have a balanced life now. This means asking myself some questions and then getting what I need, but not necessarily as much as I want.

For example - how much one to one talking do I actually need?
- Is it hearing my own voice, or sharing ideas which is important?

- Is it the fact that someone is listening which satisfies me?

- How much touching do I need to give and receive?

- Can I hug a friend every day?

- Do I need a lover?

- Will my cats purring on my lap be enough, most of the time?

- Do I want to go to parties and see many people, or do I get the kind of attention I need from one person at a time?

- Is it the quantity of encounters during the day, or week, or is it a certain kind of attention which makes life joyful enough?

- Do I want to live with someone, or with many people?

Understand what you need, and do something to get it, and give it.

Phone your friends, send email, write letters, take classes, walk in the park, get a cat, consider a different living arrangement, whatever will prevent a sense of isolation.

Listen to yourself and change your life so that these phrases are not true.

Nobody loves me.

I am of no value.

Nobody needs me.

I am unlovable.

No one would miss me if I were not here.

I have no one to love.

I am not giving anything to the world.

I don't need anyone.

Stop those nagging voices through your actions, by giving love and accepting your needs.

These ghostly refrains live in a swamp that takes effort to escape if you wander into it during low periods.

If you let it, this type of refrain can become a lingering illness which invades you as the years pass, especially as you find yourself tipping the balance toward death.

WHAT DO YOU DO if this happens to you?   Take it as a message, like dreams, or symptoms which are trying to get your attention.   You are floundering in your search to find value in what it means for you to be alive, and to understand what it means to be finite.

You and I have a limited time in our continuing search for understanding of who we are and where we are on the cycle of life and death.

Each of us is alone on our individual path.
We may find like characters whom we link
hands, hearts, and minds with along the way,
but we live with uncertainty.

We ease the human condition when

we give

and accept love .

That is our great gift to each other. We
also join with the animal kingdom for warmth
and companionship as part of our continuing
search for closeness.   Act from this
understanding, and with luck you may also
encounter Nasrudin and other wise jokers

along the way as reminders of what you really

need to thrive, if you have slipped off the

path, and as humorous relief on dark days.

It is all too easy to lie to yourself, to

deny, or to soften truths about yourself

that you may encounter. But, Lies give

you a warped sense of your world.

Distortions of reality injure your sense of

knowing, as when you are forced by your

surroundings to believe what you know is

not true, for you.

Your reality of the world begins, early in life, with what your senses are telling you, how you are touched, held, fed and loved. How you are cared for as a baby will be reflected in your feelings toward others in your world.

Children are often treated in ways they know are unjust, physically and emotionally lied to, and punished for their guardian's problems. That damage is recorded deep in each soul.

For instance, a denial of childhood sexual feelings and responses is still prevalent and leaves many scars.

Unreal religious doctrines, or abuse of any kind that we are forced to see as happening to us for our own good, are powerful examples of lies we can face and speak their names.

Lies and secrets are often related.

There are several kinds of secrets.   One kind is escaped secrets which need to be protected from destructive elements.   They have become gossip, the 'did you know' variety.   There are also ideas for creative projects which are developing, which are damaged by talking too much about them.

You need to keep them secret for as long as possible, until they are fully formed. Tell one person and they are no longer secret.

Lies need to be faced when they have been forced to become deadly secrets. Shameful secrets we carry, destroy us physically and deaden our sensitivity to our creative energies.

If you carry these secrets, you will need to find someone who can bear to hear them, who can feel your emotion, and then you can allow them to dissipate into the air.

This kind of secret poisons your life, and is usually secret only because the society you live in has decided it cannot be voiced.
Some people are afraid to hear some truths.

It is often to do with abuse of some kind from a person you are frightened of. It may be about your sexuality, gender, or religious practices.

If you are on the receiving end of secrets, choose not to pass them on, not to turn them into gossip. This silence is gallantry.

Respond like Nasrudin who,

when asked if he could keep a secret,

said he was not responsible for other

people's storage problems.

As you **Listen** to yourself and others you

will learn to hear what you and they are really

saying. Begin by listening to yourself, and

then turn to others who need someone to

hear their words as well as experience

their silences.

For example, what is hidden behind these words ?

- I don't mind if you see other women, as long as I don't know about it.

- There is nothing sexual about our cuddles.   He is just trying to comfort me.

-    We don't sleep together any more. It's really better because I sleep more soundly alone.

- I'm fine, just finding it a little hard to go to sleep, or to get up in the morning.

- Of course, I will wait until my husband finds a job he likes before I look for one. I can work anywhere.

When you hear yourself, or others, say these or similar words, making similar excuses, prick up your ears and do something about it.

ASK yourself-

Why are these sentiments coming out now?

Can anything be done to change what is happening ?

Is this a situation that has to be accepted, until other elements enter the story?

As you are talking to yourself, or listening to others talk, consider it a way to vent emotion.
It is a release valve that lowers the pitch enough to think creatively.

However, without action talking remains - just a vent.

One final question may come into your mind—

AM I CRAZY?

Mental health and mental illness are concepts that are common in western society. What do these terms mean to you and me as we look more closely at ourselves? They include a culturally specific concept of our whole body and environment, which makes it a very unique picture based on history and place.

Mental illness carries with it the fears, and facts, of misdiagnosis, mistreatment, and loss of freedom which have so often accompanied the treatment of the time. This is true especially for women within this medical model.

However, there are some of us who may be medically diagnosed as delicate, or depressed, or who feel we are not functioning well.   We choose to take pills, or are prescribed medication, perhaps not of our choosing, but the pills keep us living in the community.

We are mirrors of what is going on around us in the community, reflecting the distortions, ugliness, and pain of our world.

As mirrors, we are magnifications of the obstacles facing each person attempting to live a full life.

It is perilous for others to look away from these painful reflections, or to forget that each of us suffers within a crowded, yet often isolated environment.

To promote mental health you and I need to confront troubling questions of body and soul .

These are often left unasked because it is not fashionable, or they are thought impossible to prove, so of no importance. However, with persistence, it is possible to discover for yourself how much of this or that, including the incertitude of life, you need to be healthy.

In a healthy state your reactions are fluid and shift with each occasion.

Nasrudin understood that changing circumstances alter your reactions to situations.   On one occasion Nasrudin was seen to blow on his soup to cool it, and on other occasions, to blow on his hands to warm them.

As you progress with your self analysis you will understand the importance of enough

Struggle and Balance.

This is the legendary *razor's edge* each individual must walk as his unique path.

From birth struggle is vital and forces you to develop. No one should be denied some struggle. However, there is an optimum frustration level which keeps evolutionary tendencies working well.

Watch a baby struggling to reach a new toy. You damage the baby's confidence if you immediately hand her the toy she is making such a valiant effort to get for herself. When she finally reaches it, she will feel immense satisfaction and try the next time, even if it is further away.

Struggle
and Balance —

266

This internal balance needs careful observation.   We each have senses, emotions, feelings, intuition, and thoughts, all competing in our lives.   One of these may habitually take precedence, depending on our characteristics, and we lose our balance.

For instance, I lose my balance when I write for too many hours and do not exercise, stop to eat, to see the sunset, talk to my cat, or ring my daughters.   This leaves me feeling out of sorts. So what can I do ? I can observe myself more often, which sharpens my perceptual skills so that I can predict how I may get out of balance, and

what my personal tendencies are.   This
helps me to catch myself more quickly and I
can do something practical to get back into
balance.   I understand when I have
struggled enough, and realize I may need help
from a friend at this point.

You can go overboard and work too long, too
intensely,
even in self analysis.

Check yourself.

Enough

is the important measure when balancing and
struggling to get anything right.

Give enough attention and energy to
emotions, thoughts, and consequent
actions.
All lovers, skiers, surfers, and rock
climbers know this.

Balance in your inner life relates to its
opposite, surplus in your daily life. Surplus
and the inevitable storage problems it
creates is a major contributing factor to our
discontent as individuals, as a society, and
as a world, groaning under the weight of
rubbish and pollution.   You can do
something about your excess in every part of
your life.   Lighten your burden.

Obvious categories of excess are -

Too much food - so fat is a major concern with many of us.

Too much time on our hands - so boredom, depression, and distractions preoccupy us.

Too many things, books included – so that we have storage and disposal problems.

Have enough, only what you really need.

You leave room in your life for new actions and memories when you are slightly lean and hungry for life.

Having read this far, you have the
information to begin to heal yourself.
Your future will be a mixture of the results
of this day, your past, plus your response to
forces you do not control .

Seize the day.

An ancient story tells it –

There was once a young man, full of hope,
who set out with his ships to explore the
world, and to bring back some of its
treasures for his land and king.

A raging storm dashed his ships and his dreams on the rocks, and he was washed up on a lonely white beach, naked and unconscious.

As his luck would have it, some lovely young women were gathering shells for a ceremony the next day, when they came upon him. They bathed him in warm oil and fed him exotic fruits, as they carried him over the sand dunes to a castle near by.

A celebration was to take place the next day where a young man would be chosen as

the new king of the land.   He was new
to the country, and handsome,   so the
stranger was encouraged to enter for the
crown.   As is the way of stories, he won
the crown the castle, and all the glory he
might ever have imagined.

On the night of the celebration he
learned, from the wise man of the court,
that this title was only for one year.
His predecessor had that very morning
been put on a ship alone, and sent to a far
off island, never to return.   His
excitement was somewhat short lived at
this news.

However, as is the fortune of the young,
he recovered quickly, and set about
enjoying all the fruits of the land in a
very royal way.

As the time drew nearer for him to give
up the crown he spoke again to the wise
man, and asked if he had to be on his own
during his exile.

Was the island where he would be sent
uninhabited ?

Did it have to remain so ?

Slowly it dawned on him, that as king he was all powerful during that one year. He realised that he could prepare for his future, day by day.

When the time came for him to relinquish his crown, and step onto the small boat which would carry him to the island, far out of sight, he did so with a happy smile. He was sailing off to a magnificent palace, a well established community of all his friends, as well as members from every trade and profession necessary to enrich a long and happy life. No other king had thought of that.

Stories, through the centuries, make us smile in recognition of our common humanity and encourage you and me to seize the day, the moment.

Myths are full of warnings not to fall asleep, but to watch for signs which will allow you to pass through gates to another existence at the exact moment the guardian is asleep or looking elsewhere.

When you stay awake to catch the instant, you are seizing the day.

So, after all this,

WHAT can you do NOW?

Feel at home as who you are.

This is a good start.

However, there are a few **reminders** I always keep in my pocket for the time when I have wandered into a swamp of uncertainty.

These reminders can be separated into three areas, but they are all connected- **truth, taboos and ethics, plus your actions.**

First, ask - **whose truth** - in any

situation.

Expand your thinking to include other

perspectives, hers, his, even mine.

You cannot legalise, canonise, or politicise,

the truth.

You can only, courageously, live your

truth.

Second, free yourself from cultural

taboos as you recognize them for the

restricting forces they are.

They are your personal dragons.

We know our prejudices and hatred have
been taught to us.
Broaden the spectrum of avenues down which
to walk, in any country, by refusing to be
fenced in by dogma and fear.
Choose to look into your open heart, as a
mirror of who you are and decide on the
ethics which mean something to you.

Third, ask yourself if what you are doing
is necessary, appropriate, and for whom.

For instance, on a very practical level
Is my son able to do his own laundry and
feed himself, occasionally ?

whose necessity?
examine your life!

stopping The birds from flying

Do I need to drive my children to school, and to after school lessons every day ?

Do I need six locks on my new metal door to be safe ?

Do I respond to lovers and friends from my necessity or theirs ?

What do I need to do for myself and those I love to have a flourishing life ?

What do I need to encourage them to do for themselves ?

Be persistent, and turn these questions into

appropriate action.

When I am temporarily lost I hunt for Nasrudin

and other jokers I have met to bring me back on

the road of humour.

This is the time to close the book, build,

and push out your own boat and see if it

floats, as Jung suggested to each of us.

Learn from the past, the one you have lived,

as well as what has been handed down in oral

and written legends and history.

At the same time, develop your own 21st century method of educated self analysis. I refer back to Freud and his important role in self analysis because his work calls forth respect for his never ending belief in combined practice and research.

Freud and his colleagues made terrible errors of judgment in their medical practice. However, through his beautifully written case studies, we can read and learn for ourselves.

You can kid yourself that you are doing something in your intellectual pursuit of

more knowledge.   But only when you close
the manual and experience self analysis
will you know for yourself.

However, if you want to know more about
Freud, ,Jung, Psychoanalysis, and
Creative Art and Sand Play
therapies -
read the concluding section.
It never hurts to know the background
to your subject.

As has been said in Tibet -
recognition
and
illumination are simultaneous

PAUSE AND CONSIDER

If you decide you want support from someone who has been down the path, before you strike out on your own, here is some Foundation and Background information for the road.

Paths others have taken.

Let's start with Freud's story.

If you choose an analytical path, remember Freud and Jung both did it and lived to write volumes.

You can take yourself apart and still exist. You will learn how to reassemble yourself bit by bit as issues come into your life. There are ways. Yours is a unique adventure.

Sigmund FREUD (1856-1939) is an inspiration because of his determination to know himself and because he was the first to analyse himself and give it a name. He became a model of how and why to proceed. Several crises, all came together in a series of disturbing dreams, compelling him to act, to delve into his unconscious for understanding.

He experienced what were for him major changes - his age of 39, as well as a turning point in his professional life, and then he suffered a great loss when his father died.

Alongside his personal analysis he also studied his patients, ancient myths, and archeology, from which he learned about daily life, symbols, and pathways necessary when digging into the past.   He saw reflections of himself in everything he studied.   For many years he recorded his journey, fully and painfully, in letters to his friend Wilhelm Fleiss.

The culmination of his self analysis, and the end to his grieving over his father, came when Freud completed *The Interpretation of Dreams (1900).* This book plus his unique case studies are a courageous legacy of his trials, errors, and willingness to let the world see them.

Freud was a consummate action analyst, he acted on his theories. He left us a picture of symptoms, as clues on a map leading to treasure. They were tentative threads leading to some forgotten trauma.

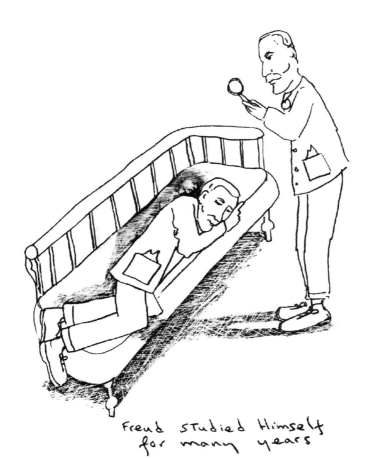

Freud studied Himself
for many years

The value of what Freud did is found in the persistent searching, and the insights he got along the way into the needs and workings of the human heart and soul - a torch he left for each one of us to keep alight.

Freud also HEARD Women FOR THE FIRST TIME IN THEIR LIVES. They gained the courage to voice their stories because he listened.   Women went on to tell their stories to friends, lovers, and others, and they learned to listen as well. In the late 19th century they slowly let the world know that what was going on behind closed doors in

Vienna, was also going on all over the western world.   Women had been labeled hysterical. They had been silenced, and restricted, in their communities, because they were women.

Revealing these secrets helped to free their energies and heal their spirits, and then their symptoms. Their revelations gave them courage to change what they could, and to encourage the next generations to continue working for inner freedom, and outward recognition.

Carl JUNG (1875-1961) was a disciple of Freud for several years. He was chosen to take on Freud's mantle, until Jung decided that, in spite of their many agreements, their differences were too great.

They had both spent years in self analysis, due to personal dramas and crises in their lives. However, shortly after the break with Freud, Jung plunged into his fantasies and dreams where the characters he encountered in his inner search unleashed new forces within him. He was determined to know what was going on in his unconscious, even to the edge of psychosis, but he kept a firm hold on reality through his family and work.

He studied alchemy intensively. It became for him a bridge between ancient thinkers and modern psychology, which he was helping to develop. He studied the symbolic alchemical transformation of base metal into gold, and the union of the opposites, that produces something more than the two parts within each individual. This union represented what was happening to him.

Jung came to realise the importance of the hidden feminine in the unconscious of men, that was necessary to make them whole, and the opposite case in women.

He observed that new ideas and creativity are not a product of will power, but that they arrive as gifts from our unconscious, when we are receptive.

Jung observed in his own life how the material world is full of life, and reacts with your unconscious when you are distressed or fragmented. For example, things seem to fly out of your hands, or hide from you, when you are in this state. Notice your inability to park your car in a huge space on some days.

Jung devoted nearly four years to looking inward and demanding answers from his unconscious.

This left him with material for his entire life study.   Jung felt that his search was necessary in order for him to live.

His self analysis was a model of creative thinking, combined with great necessity and persistence, which produced continuous work on himself and with others.   He was the narrator and director in his creative work, and just as he had developed his own personal method of working, he insisted others develop theirs.   Jung would not allow people to climb on his boat if he could stop them. He stressed that it is infinitely more creative to sail your own ship.

Jung looked for continuous transformation and creative achievement throughout his lifetime. This is the essence of self analysis - inner process combined with action .

He is an inspiration for me because his work, his writing, his life, were all one. It did not matter to him whether his story was true for others, or matched some philosophical ideal. Jung lived his personal myth. It was his truth. Finding your personal myth and your truth is what this process is all about.

Freud and Jung developed

PSYCHOANALYSIS in the late 19th and

early 20th centuries.

If you embark on psychoanalysis you will make a commitment to honest dialogue, an unwritten contract between the two people involved, which implies speaking what is truthful, as far as you know it, and listening with your total being to the words of the other.   Absolute candor is required.

Psychoanalysis emphasises the importance of looking at physical symptoms and undercurrents in your daily life and sleep caused by unrecognized internal disturbance.

If you choose to take this route here are some tips.

Special attention is given to resistances that crop up during sessions which are trying to stop the process. Resistances are safety devices to keep behaving in familiar ways. Even behaviour you insist you are trying to change can suddenly seem worth keeping.

Excuses of all kinds come into your mind for not doing things you said you intended to, in the previous session. Trickery and deception can seem to take over your thinking and talking.

This can be very distressing for you, and your analyst, to watch.   You become like a child who wants just one more glass of water, one cuddle more, the door a bit more open, another light on, before giving into the inevitable changes sleep brings.

You may temporarily feel worse, as unpleasant feelings and thoughts begin to surface, or you may develop new symptoms. Change of any kind means different and new, and that is scary.

The analyst will also be aware of the **attachment** you may feel toward her, and she toward you.   These often mirror unfinished relationship business from the past that we each use as a kind of template for relationships we have now.   We repeat and repeat emotional experiences which have not been resolved, in an attempt to get it right this time.   This attachment is seem by some philosophical thinkers to be an attempt to form a connection which goes deep in each soul, perhaps even to your personal goddess or god figure.   It is to be handled with extreme sensitivity by each person because of its great value.

The delicate connection
between therapist and client.

301

You may assume, rightly or wrongly, that the analyst possesses greater understanding in some areas where you are lacking. After all, you are entrusting your most intimate thoughts and feelings to this person. As with a doctor, there is always the idea of being in her hands.

All of these possibilities can make a complicated relationship develop, and each party needs to be aware of that. However, given the proper care, attention, time, and reality, a deep and trusting relationship can develop for the benefit of both people.

Dreams are often analysed in depth, using free association, to see how each part of the dream connects or leads on to other images. As in earlier discussion of dream interpretation, you must feel it to be right.

When you are deciding on an analyst, it is worth checking that one of the goals of your psychoanalysis will be to learn this process for yourself. You may want clarification, from time to time, and benefit from an open door policy on the part of the analyst.

The final tip is -

LEAVE IF YOU NEED TO.

Don't ever stay with a therapist when you

feel something is wrong for you.

Leave, then find a person, or another way,

which is right for you.

You might decide to investigate

Creative Therapies

which encourage artistic expression and are

mainly silent, in contrast to talking therapies.

What you produce in these creative moments with paint, or by some other artistic medium of your choice, are often pathways to your deepest thoughts.   As you see your creations laid out before you, your words can become clear and flow easily.

Experiencing the process, with some support and guidance when you want it, means you can safely catch yourself at game playing, kidding yourself, lying, denying and sometimes not doing what you think you are doing, and not saying what you mean.

You can take a clear look at what the imaginary cartoon bubble above your head would say, if you were telling the truth.

ART THERAPY

is essentially a non verbal tool of self discovery which looks at what you put into, or leave out of, both spontaneous painting and your life.

ART THERAPY

A session with a therapist may go like this.

You draw a picture.

It is quickly drawn.

Looking at it you are surprised by what you see.

You did not intend to put blue there, but you did.

You meant to draw a tiger, but you drew a bear instead.

Who and where are you in the painting, or are you there?

Look carefully and see your intentions.

What you draw, or leave out of your

painting, is similar to what you

include or leave out of other areas in

your daily life.

Saying -   I didn't mean to, but . . .

I don't want to cry all the time, but. . .

I love her , him, mother, father, but. . . .

each suggests you could be more accurate, as

well as honest or brave, with yourself.

So, what stops your good intentions from

being transformed into actions?   You do.

You meant to draw a tiger, but didn't.

Why don't you do what you intend ?

In the picture it doesn't matter, but in life if your intentions don't match your actions, then you are sabotaging yourself? Looking at yourself in this way you may have natural resistances to digging in painful areas, so to be certain you reach your inner core, you can trick your censors in order to pass into your personal underworld.

Art can be the necessary trick and this action can move you to see previously unseen connections, because they are down in paint and you can't pretend.   They are there, or left out.

Begin to paint, or to find again your
paintbrush laid down long ago, and make
your life full of lost or forgotten colour.
Parts of yourself may have been
misplaced, or through necessity hidden
from the world.

You set your imagination free in this
way.

Someone who has been there before you can
help you see how these patterns in paint
correspond to your patterns in life, but you
can do it on your own.

There is no judgment of your painting skills or of what you find.   No one else knows what shapes, or colours mean to you.   There is no interpretation, only noticing for yourself, catching your tricks.

Another, related, way to get in touch with hidden parts of your self is SAND PLAY.

Sand has enchanted me since childhood. It fills the magical space between the deep sea, the crashing waves, and the chaotic, material world.

Sand play is for you - IF

you want - to explore and expand your
creativity,
to look more deeply into a problem,
to be more visual than verbal,
or simply to make time for this kind of play.

The therapist will have a special room, lined
with shelves, full of miniatures representing
your outer life - cars, trees, bridges,
houses, figures of all kinds.

Your inner quest may also be represented by
glass shapes, rocks, shells, beads, and
abstract forms.

You creatively portray in your
constructions what you might not be able
to portray with words, until you have seen
it in the sand first.

The process goes something like this-
Focus on the shelves of objects, and you will
learn to leave censoring, questioning, and
expectations out of this process.
Choose pieces which speak out or catch your
eye and place them in the sand box.
Shape the sand to your imagination.
Expose the blue sea.   Sail your ships.
Fight dragons.   Build castles, or trek across
the desert to an oasis.

Some sand constructions will flow easily. Others will seem incomprehensible at the time.   No two will ever be the same.   The process will take 20 to 40 minutes to complete to your satisfaction.

It is a symbolic process of creation that holds the keys to unlocking many imaginative and forgotten doors.

You will soon feel comfortable with the therapist, who is there quietly, as a holding presence, and possible co explorer with you, should you want companionship.

Sand play enables healing through delayed interpretation, and deliberate discouragement of rational thought.

First you create.

Then you may talk about it, or not.

It is after the creative act, that you begin to see the difference between what you say and what you do.

Only you know what the constructions mean. You will experience an internal transformation through a series of sand plays, and through your connection to the deepest parts of your self.

Each sand play is photographed on completion, and after a series, lasting from a few weeks to a few months, a photographic slide analysis will be arranged. This gives you a chance to look at what you have created, from a distance, and to assess the value of the process for yourself. You will see periods of stillness, waiting for some as yet unconscious perception to emerge, as well as periods of inner conflict and new inner strengths emerging.

This is truly a wonderful, creative door through which adults, and children, step with equal satisfaction.

A Consultant Counsellor can be a temporary solace and encourage you to proceed further on your own.

When symptoms block your life, disturb your sleep, give you mysterious pains and aches, and you can't sort it out, it is time to talk to someone who has walked this way before you, trying to make sense of life. This counsellor, like you is searching for clues along the way.

As you enter this relationship you may ask, why me, why now, but the answer is clear.

You search for meaning, when you have to.

You need to be ready to bare your soul to this person because your need to hear your story, and to see your story, is greater for this time than your fear of exposure. The counsellor honours your confidentiality, hears your words, experiences your silences.

You tell your truth, not an ideal truth, or her truth. She will listen to the best of her ability, and give support and guidance as you hone your skills and pick up hints, much like taking a master class. However, you will be doing the work, gathering strength to go solo.

Freud did not speak of cure during analysis, but of understanding the nature of our discontent which makes it possible to work and to love. To have both of these in your life is a rich reward for the difficult tasks in self searching.

If, in the end, you have chosen to find your own path, to do it by yourself, remember that ANALYSIS and ACTION alternate in this play.

In **self analysis** you are engaged in an intellectual and practical process of taking apart your components and seeing what makes you tick in your unique way.

You do this because you are curious, interested in preventive action, or something is wrong.

Analysing your actions helps you to expand your thinking and deepen your perceptions of what is possible for you.

By the time you decide 'enough already' , more gazing inward, for the moment, you will have developed a more philosophical understanding of your problems because you have dared to look and see yourself more clearly in relation to those around you, and to what we glibly call our global village. What you have seen you can no longer not see.

Take a DEEP BREATH
now, before the EPILOGUE

As for who I am now - this will hopefully be
evident from what I have written.

Who I was, what I did, where I studied,
where I lived, with whom I lived - are all
screen memories that are as shifting as the
sands of Cancun beach.

Each time I recall a different part of the
story, just as you do.

My thoughts and actions are seen now, in
writing these words.

You are on your way.

Good Luck

Suggested Reading

SELF ANALYSIS

Anzieu, Didier (1975), Freud's Self-Analysis. A smaller version]n one volume. Self Analysis, Its Role in Freud's Discovery of Psychoanalysis, 1959. A second version, changed and enlarged, published in two volumes by Presses Universitaires de France, 1975. The English translation by Peter Graham, Edited by Clifford Yorke. Present edition, one volume, is taken from the second version minus many Appendices already in English publications). London: The Hogarth Press Ltd., (1986).

Anzieu, Didier (1993), 'Beckett, Self-Analysis and Creativity', translated by Pierre Johannet, taken from Self-Analysis, edited by James Barron. Hillsdale, New Jersey: The Analytic Press.

Barron, James W. (1993) Editor, Self-Analysis (Critical Inquires, Personal Visions). Hillsdale, New Jersey: The Analytic Press.

Cooper, Arnold M. (1996) 'Foreward', taken from What Do Analysts Want?, written by Joseph Sandler and Anna Ursula Drehfer. Editor, Elizabeth Bott Spillius, 'The New Library of Psychoanalysis', Number 24. London: Routledge (in association with The Institute of Psycho-Analysis, London).

Demos, E. Virginia (1993), 'Capacity for Self-Analysis', taken from Self-Analysis, Edited by James Barron. Hillsdale, New Jersey: The Analytic Press.

Horney, Karen (1942), Self-Analysis. London: Routledge & Kegan Paul Ltd., Paperback (1962).

Lussier, Martine (1993), 'Freud's Self-Analysis', taken from Self-Analysis, Edited by James Barron. Hillsdale, New Jersey: The Analytic Press.

Margulies, Alfred (1993), 'The Mirror of the Other', taken from Self-Analysis,

Edited by James Barron. Hillsdale, New Jersey: The Analytic Press.

Masson, Jeffrey Moussaieff (1985), Translator and Editor, The Complete Letters of Sigmund Freud to Wilhelm Fliess 1887-1904. Cambridge, Ma., and London: The Belknap Press of Harvard University Press.

Miller, Alice (1985), Pictures of a Childhood, originally in German. First published in English 1985/1986, Farrar Straus and Girous Ins., New York. British edition, London: Virago Press Ltd. (1995).
Milner, Marion (1937), An Experiment in Leisure. London: Virago Press Ltd. (1988).

Mitchell, Stephen A. (1993), 'Forword', taken from Self Analysis, Edited by James Barron. Hillsdale, New Jersey: The Analytic Press. Neumann, Erich (1954), 'Creative Man and Transformation', Previously published Eranos-Jahrbuch. Art and the Creative Unconscious (1959). Bollingen Series LXI, Princeton, New Jersey: Princeton University Press, Bollingen Paperback Edition 1971 (Third printing, 1974).

Poland, Warren (1993), 'Self and Other in Self-Analysis', taken from Self-Analysis, Edited by James Barron. Hillsdale, New Jersey: The Analytic Press.

Sandler, Joseph and Anna Ursula Dreher (1996), What Do Analysts Want? Editor, Elizabeth Bott Spillius. London: Routledge (in association with The Institute of Psycho-Analysis, London).

Wolf, Ernest S. (1993), 'Self-Analysis of a Taboo', taken from Self-Analysis, Edited by James Barron. Hillsdale, New Jersey: The Analytic Press.

FREUD

Appignanesi, Richard, and Oscar Zarate (1992), Freud for Beginners. Cambridge: Icon Books.
Ellenberger, Henri F. (1970), The Discovery of the Unconscious. London: Fontana Press (1994).

Ellman, Steven J.(1991), Freud's Technique Papers, A Contemporary Perspective. New Jersey: Jason Aronson Inc.

Erickson, E.A. (1949), 'The Dream Specimen of Psychoanalysis'. (Publisher unclear).

Freud, Sigmund and Joseph Breuer (1895), Studies on Hysteria. London: Penguin Books (1974/1991 reprint).

Freud, Sigmund (1900), The Interpretation of Dreams, translated by James Strachey. London: Penguin Books Ltd., Pelican Freud Library edition (1982).

Freud, Sigmund (1905), 'Fragment of an analysis of a case of hysteria', Standard Edition, Volume 7. London: Hogarth Press (1953).

Freud, Sigmund (1912), 'The Dynamics of the Transference', Standard Edition,
Vol 2. London: Hogarth Press (1958).

Freud, Sigmund (1914), 'Remembering, Repeating and Working-Through', Standard Edition, Volume 12. London: Hogarth Press (1958).

Freud, Sigmund (1916/1917), 'Introductory Lectures on Psycho-Analysis', Standard Edition, Volumes 15-16. London: Hogarth Press (1963).

Freud, Sigmund (1921), Group Psychology and the Analysis of the Ego. New York: Bantam Books edition, (1965).

Freud, Sigmund (1930), Civilization and its Discontents. London: The Hogarth Press (1969).

Freud, Sigmund (1937), 'Analysis Terminable and Interminable', Standard Edition, Volume 23. Longon: Hogarth Press (1964).

Gay, Peter (1988), Freud, A Life for Our Time. London: Papermac (1989).

Jones, Ernest (1953), The Life and Work of Sigmund Freud, Edited and abridged in one volume by Lionel Trilling and Steven Marcus. London: Pelican Books (1964).

Paskauskas, Andrew R., Editor (1993), The Complete Correspondence of Sigmund Freud and Ernest Jones 1908-1939. Cambridge, MA: The Belknap Press Harvard University Press.

JUNG

Battye, Nicholas (1994), 'Khidr in the Opus of Jung:
The Teaching of Surrender'. From, Joel Ryce-
Menuhin, Editor (1994), Jung and the Monotheisms.
Judaism, Christianity, and Islam. London: Routledge.

Begg, Ean (1983), 'Gnosis and the Single Vision', from
In the Wake of Jung, A Selection from 'Harvest',
Molly Tuby (Editor). London: Coventure Ltd.

Hyde, Maggie, and Michael McGuinness (1992), Jung for
Beginners, Cambridge: Icon Books Ltd.

Jacobi, Jolande (1939), The Psychology of C.G. Jung.
London: Routledge & Kegan Paul, (Seventh edition,
Reprinted 1980).

Jung, C.G. (1909), The Freud/Jung Letters: The
Correspondence between Sigmund Freud and C.G. Jung.
Princeton: Princeton University Press (1974).

Jung, C.G. (1922), 'On the Relation of Analytical
Psychology to Poetry', Translated from 'Uber Die
Beziehungen der analytischen Psychologie zum
dichterischen Kuntwerk', Seelenprobleme der
Gegenwart, (Zurich: Rascher, 1931). London: Ark
Paperbacks (1984 Edition, Reprinted 1993).

Jung, C.G. (1933), Modern Man in Search of a Soul, New York: Harcourt, Brace & World, Inc.

Jung, C.G. (1935), Analytical Psychology Its Theory and Practice. London: Ark Paperbacks (1986)

Jung, C.G. (1945), C.G. Jung Psychological Reflections, An Anthology of His Writings 1905-1961, Selected and Edited by Jolande Jacobi, (First edition in English 1953). London: Ark Paperbacks (1986).

Jung, C.G. (1946), The Psychology of the Transference, London: Ark Paperbacks (1983).

Jung, C.G. (1946a), 'On the Nature of the Psyche', (Revised edition 1954), Bollingen Series XX, also in The Collected Works of C.G. Jung, Volume 8. New Jersey: Princeton University Press.

Jung, C.G. (1950), 'A Study in the Process of Individuation', Translated from 'Zur Empirie des Individuationsprozesses', Gestaltungen des Unbewussten, (Zurich: Rascher, 1950). (Revised, enlarged version, first published in 1933/34 in Eranos-Jahrbuch, Eds. note p.6). Mandala Symbolism, (1972). New Jersey: Princeton University Press, (Bollingen series, paperback).

Jung, C.G. (1950), 'Concerning Mandala Symbolism', Translated from 'Uber Mandalasymbolid', GestTaltungen des Unbewussten (Zurich: Rascher, 1950), Illustrations

first gathered for a seminar which Jung gave in Berlin in 1930. Mandala Symbolism, (1972).
New Jersey: Princeton University Press, (Bollingen series, paperback).

Jung, C.G. (1953), Psychology and Alchemy, Second Edition, revised (1968). Material from two lectures published in Eranos-Jahrbuch 1935 & 1936, later in Zurich 1936 & 1937. After 1940 they were expanded. Published in German, Zurich: Rascher Verlag, 1944, 2nd Edition, revised, 1952. Number 12 of the Collected Works. London: Routledge paperback (1993).

Jung, C.G. (1954), Answer to Job. London: Ark Paperbacks (1984).

Jung, C.G. (1961), Memories, Dreams, and Reflections, (Book had its inception at Ascona 1956, completed 1961, Recorded and Edited by Aniela Jaffe, Translated from German by Richard and Clara Winston, First published in Great Britain by Collins and Routledge & Kegan Paul, 1963. London: Collins, The Fontana Library of Theology and Philosophy (Fifth impression, 1972).

Wilhelm, Richard/ Jung, C.G., Foreword and Commentary (1931), The Secret of the Golden Flower, A Chinese Book of Life. (German Edition 1929, new revised edition 1962.) London: Arkana Paperbacks (1984).

ART THERAPY

Adamson, Edward (1990), Art as Healing. London: Coventure Ltd.

Silverstone, Liesl (1993), Art Therapy - the Person-Centred Way.London:Autonomy Books.

SANDPLAY THERAPY

Kalff, Dora M. (1980), Sandplay: A Psychotherapeutic Approach to the Psyche, Originally published in German 1979, as Sandspiel: Seine therapeutische Wirkung auf die Psyche. English translation by Hilde Kirsch and Wendayne Ackermann. English edition first published 1981. Boston, Massachusetts: Sigo Press (Second printing, 1986).

Mitchell, Rie Rogers, & Harriet S. Friedman (1994), Sandplay: Past, present and future. London: Routledge. Ryce-Menuhin, Joel (1992), Jungian Sandplay: The wonderful therapy. London: Routledge.

Weinrib, Estelle L. (1983), Images of the Self: The Sandplay Therapy Process. Massachusetts: Sigo Press.

OTHER

Becker, Ernest (1973), The Denial of Death, New York: The Free Press, (1975 Paperback).

Brown, Norman O. (1959), Life Against Death: The Psychoanalytic Meaning of History, New York: Viking Books.

Galland, China (1998), A Bond Between Women: A Journey of Fierce Compassion. New York: Riverhead Books (Penguin Putnam Inc.)

Karma-glin-pa, 14th cent., The Tibetan book of the dead : the great liberation through hearing in the Bardo / by Guru Rimpoche according to Karma Lingpa p a new translation with commentary by Francesca Fremantle and Chogyam Trungpa. Berkeley: Shambhala (1975). This edition Boston: Massachusetts.

Laplanche, J. and J.B. Pontalis (1967), The Language of Psychoanalysis. Original French edition, Vocabularie de la Psychoanalyse, published by Presses Universitaires de France 1967. English translation by Donald Nicholson-Smith, published by Hogarth Press Ltd., 1973. This Edition London: The Institute of Psychoanalysis and Karnac Books (1988).

Miller, Alice (1990), Breaking Down the Wall of Silence to Join the Waiting Child. Translated from German by Simon Worrall. London: Virago Press (1991).

Nussbaum, Martha C. (1994), The Therapy of Desire, Theory and Practice in Hellenistic Ethics. New Jersey: Princeton University Press.

Stettbacher, J. Konrad (1990), Making Sense of Suffering, The Healing Confrontation with Your Own Past. Foreword and afterword by Alice Miller: translated by Simon Worrall. Originally published in German as 'Wenn Leiden einen Sinn haben Soll', by Hoffmann and Campe Verlag, Hambury. New York: Dutton/Division of Penguin Books USA Inc. (1991).

Thurman, Robert A.F. (1994), The Tibetan Book of the Dead. Known in Tibet as - The Great Book of Natural Liberation Through Understanding in the Between. Composed by Padma Sambhave. Discovered by Karma Lingpa. London: Harper Collins, (Imprint Thorsons).

Von Franz, Marie-Louise (1979), Alchemical Active Imagination. Dallas, Texas: Spring Publications Inc.

TAPE RECORDINGS - Joseph Campbell,

(1990), Transformations of Myth Through Time, Vol. 1-3. Recording: Highbridge Productions, St.Paul, MIN, U.S.A.

ABOUT US
illustrator and author

Myrna Shoa is a British painter and storyteller who studied painting at the Royal College of Art London, where she gained her M.A.

Myrna designs and makes greeting cards that she sells from her shop in the Portobello Road, London. The designs are based upon personal and traditional stories.   She has also written and illustrated a book of stories for children.

Email - MshoaCards@aol.com

Author

I call myself a philosophical practitioner and counsellor, using the therapeutic techniques of art and sand play.   I am a member of the teaching staff, in counselling, at the Institute of Sexuality and Human Relations, in London.   I have received a B.A. degree in Criminology and an M. A. in Psychoanalysis.

Born in Hollywood, I am also British.   My personal experience comes from living half my life in different cultures and observing individuals and families around me with differing philosophies and religious beliefs.

Before coming to live in England in 1980, I lived for several years in Greece, and for the odd year in Italy, Lebanon, and Nigeria.

Throughout my travels and whether I was working with women or men in jail in Massachusetts, or with women escaping violent partners in a refuge in London, my main interest has been in why we do what we do, and how we can reform our experiences into new, creative actions for a flourishing life.

c.joel elva & m.shoa   c 1999
truck stop spirituality 2000
magdalena productions

The return of the goddess

is next?

Watch for the coming project.

I am currently researching a book on the return of the goddess as a vital part of psychological and spiritual life in the new millennium.   Both male and female psyches have suffered from thousands of years of her absence in many cultures.   It is not enough to have only the purity of the virgin, as in Christianity, because we are not only pure.   We need the dark side of our nature personified, in order to be whole.

Email – Create2001@aol.com

340

My NOTE - of Gratitude

The **stories** which I have retold were first inspired by hearing them told by Aury Shoa, hour after hour, and then by other friends who were storytellers, over many years. My interest was kept alive through reading the ancient tales of Sufi masters, as well as the many books of the late Idris Shah. Versions of the stories vary from country to country, but hopefully the message does not get lost as they are handed down.

Many thanks to Myrna Shoa for inspired conversations and illustrations as well as for the original - *Going To Do* - story from which the printed one was adapted.

A toast to those who made me consider including some punctuation, and to friends who have patiently read the various versions as the book evolved, especially Robyn, Michael and the One who provided my keyboard along with other valuables.

Thank you from the bottom of my heart.

note page -

ISBN 0-9538820-1-2

9 780953 882014